TIBETAN
BUDDHIST LIFE

ནང་ཆོས་ལ་བསྟེན་པའི་བོད་པའི་མི་ཚེ།

TIBETAN
BUDDHIST LIFE

DON FARBER

IN ASSOCIATION WITH
THE TIBET FUND

DK PUBLISHING

LONDON, NEW YORK, MUNICH,
MELBOURNE, and DELHI

DK PUBLISHING
Senior Editor Barbara Berger
Art Director Dirk Kaufman
Interior Design Oxygen Design,
    Sherry Williams and Tilman Reitzle
Cowriter Rebecca Novick McClen
Publisher Chuck Lang
Creative Director Tina Vaughan
Project Director Sharon Lucas
Production Manager Chris Avgherinos
DTP Designer Milos Orlovic
Contributing Writer Jennifer Williams
Calligraphy Lobsong Tsultrim
Editorial Consultants Dorji Kunthup, Joanie Choderow
Editorial Assistant John Searcy

10 9 8 7 6 5 4 3 2 1

Published in Great Britain in 2003 by
Dorling Kindersley Limited
80 Strand, London WC2R ORL

A Penguin company

A CIP catalogue record for this book is available
from the British Library.

ISBN 1-4053-0150-3

Colour reproduction by ColourScan, Singapore
Printed and bound in Italy by L.E.G.O.

See our complete product line at
www.dk.com

CONTENTS

> "In the face of great hardship, Tibetans inside and outside Tibet have achieved much to be justifiably proud of. . . . We have a responsibility to preserve our living culture, not just to our brothers and sisters in Tibet, but also to the world at large."
>
> —His Holiness the 14th Dalai Lama

INTRODUCTION
DON FARBER

A sand mandala made during the Vajrakilaya Initiation ceremony, performed by His Holiness Sakya Trizin at Sakya Center, Rajpur, 1997.

I WAS FIRST INTRODUCED to Buddhism 30 years ago, when I attended a seminar by Chogyam Trungpa Rinpoche. After studying Buddhism with my late teacher, the Vietnamese Zen master Thich Thien-An, and photographing at the Vietnamese Buddhist Temple for ten years in Los Angeles, I began studying Tibetan Buddhism with Dr. Thien-An's close friend, Geshe Tsultim Gyeltsen. Then in 1986, I had the opportunity to attend teachings by Kalu Rinpoche in Santa Fe, New Mexico. As I studied Tibetan Buddhism, I found its explanations of the nature of reality and spiritual truths incredibly profound, and I decided to focus my efforts on photographing and researching Tibetan Buddhist life. Since photographing Kalu Rinpoche's funeral in 1989, one of the most

His Holiness the Dalai Lama, *in his residence at Dharamsala, 1997.*

profound experiences of my career, I have made an ongoing photographic project of Tibetan Buddhist masters—something that I continue to do today.

I married a Tibetan woman, Yeshi Chozom, whom I met in Los Angeles, and after spending a number of years photographing Buddhist life in Asia, I obtained a Fulbright grant to photograph and research Tibetan Buddhist life in India and Nepal. In 1996, my wife and our young daughter, Tsering Palmo, went to live in my wife's village in Himachal Pradesh, India. For the next ten months, I lived with the Tibetan people and visited many Tibetan settlements with a wonderful guide and companion, my wife's brother, Lhundup. I remember a fellow in my wife's village whom the locals had nicknamed "the singing man." He walked through the village every day singing Tibetan folk songs—a scene that I found deeply moving and poignant. His voice, combined with the sounds of the horns from the monasteries that permeated the village, made a deep impression on me. I felt that this visionary culture, with its advanced spiritual understanding, was something precious that needs to be protected, nurtured, and supported. There are so many problems in the world and so many situations beyond our control, but I felt that if we could help one country and its people to continue into the future, here is one to work for. It was in this spirit that this book was born.

Soman Dolma with her grandaughter, in Himachal Pradesh, India, 1997.

At the invitation of His Holiness the Dalai Lama, I photographed him at his residence in Dharamsala. During a quiet moment as His Holiness was standing by the window, I found myself telling him the story of my wife's mother, Lhaga. Soon after Yeshi's parents escaped into North India in 1959, her mother developed paralysis in her legs. It was discovered that she had contracted polio, a disease that was virtually unknown in Tibet. The love between Lhaga and her husband, Wangyal, was so strong, however, that they went on to bear two children—my wife, Yeshi, and her younger brother, Lhundup.

A prayer festival called Nyingma Monlam is held for two weeks each year in Bodhgaya, India. Monks and nuns of the Nyingma school of Tibetan Buddhism gather to pray for world peace. Above, the 1997 Nyingma Monlam.

Two child monks who are brothers, embrace at Sonada Monastery, near Darjeeling, India, during Kalu Rinpoche's funeral, 1989.

His Holiness the Dalai Lama gave a *Kalachakra Initiation near Siliguri, India, in 1997, to the largest audience ever to attend a Kalachakra empowerment—over 250,000 people. These monks are wearing face masks to protect against dust.*

One day, the family was visiting some hot springs, and were spotted by Taring Amala, the founder of the Tibetan Homes Foundation. She was so touched by the scene of this beautiful young woman being carried on her husband's back that she invited them to come and stay at the school that she established for Tibetan orphans. She offered Wangyal a job as caretaker, and gave Yeshi and Lhundup a place in the school. When I told this story to His Holiness, he was deeply moved. "All the Tibetan people have suffered so much," he said sadly.

Through my photographic work with the Tibetan people, I came to know Rinchen Dharlo, president of the Tibet Fund. When I found out that DK Publishing wanted to give a portion of the proceeds from the sale of the book to a Tibetan organization, I recommended the Tibet Fund, which is the official relief agency established by the Tibetan Government-in-Exile. This organization is doing important work to aid Tibetan refugees in India, Nepal, and Tibet, and it is a great honor to be working with them. There are also other notable Tibet support groups who are helping Tibetans in different ways, and some of these organizations are listed in the back of this book. The lack of clean water, sanitation, and health care services within the refugee settlements means that many Tibetans are dying in their fifties, often from diseases that could have been treated but which for years went

Nuns debate at the Jangchub Choeling Monastery in Mundgod, southern India, 1997.

undiagnosed. One of the things that has become clear to me is the simple fact that in order to keep the Tibetan culture alive, the people themselves must be helped to survive.

When I married a Tibetan woman, I also married into Tibetan culture, and developed close friendships with many Tibetans. I have learned of the struggles they face, from the loss and destruction of their homeland to the difficulties of exile in India and Nepal, and the challenges of trying to make a productive life in the West. I have tremendous respect for the courage and fortitude the Tibetan people show in adversity, and have felt deeply enriched through my exposure to their culture and spirituality. I feel that so much of Tibetan Buddhism is a way of life, not just a philosophy or a system of beliefs. I hope that this book can give a taste of this, and inspire readers to get to know more about these remarkable people, their culture, and their spiritual traditions.

A funeral procession of Kagyu monks, on the 49th day of Kalu Rinpoche's funeral, Sonada Monastery, Darjeeling, India, 1989.

Four Tibetan Buddhists practice mani, 1997, during a spiritual retreat in a home for the elderly at Palyul Namdroling Monastery in Bylakuppe, India, which is near a large Tibetan settlement.

DEVELOPMENT OF TIBETAN BUDDHISM

MORE THAN 2,500 YEARS AGO, Shakyamuni Buddha attained enlightenment after many years of intensive spiritual practice, inspiring the development of one of the world's great religions. The Buddhist path is traditionally divided into three *yanas* or vehicles: Hinayana, Mahayana, and Vajrayana. The Hinayana schools, of which only Theravada remains, focuses primarily on the discourses of Shakyamuni Buddha, including his guidance to develop meditative awareness and to cease all negative emotions and actions that bind us, lifetime after lifetime, to this suffering existence called *samsara*. Mahayana includes much of what is taught in Hinayana, but it emphasizes the altruistic motivation for practitioners to attain complete enlightenment in order to save all sentient beings from suffering. The third vehicle, Vajrayana or *tantra*, means "continuum" or "unbroken stream" from ignorance to enlightenment. Vajrayana is a continuation of Hinayana and Mahayana and has been passed on through initiations from masters to disciples. In Tibetan Buddhism, all three vehicles become a single path.

Sarnath, near Varanasi, *is one of India's great Buddhist holy places. It was here that the Buddha gave his first teachings, The Four Noble Truths, and was later the site of a great monastery, now in ruins.*

ROOTS OF TIBETAN BUDDHISM

Buddhism flourished in India from the birth of Buddha in the 5th or 6th century BC to the 12th century AD, and during this time many extraordinary masters steadfastly followed the Buddha's path and attained enlightenment. These masters wrote commentaries that expanded on the Buddha's teachings, some of which had a profound effect on the development of Buddhism in Tibet.

BUDDHIST MASTERS & NALANDA UNIVERSITY

Nagarjuna was a master who lived in the 2nd century AD and is credited with the establishment of the Madhyamika or "Middle Way" school of Mahayana Buddhism, which strongly influenced the development of Tibetan Buddhism. During the 5th century, Nalanda University—the greatest center of monastic education in India—was erected in Bihar, near where Shakyamuni Buddha gave the first Mahayana teachings, and on the site where one of his disciples, Shariputra, had died. One of Nalanda's luminaries, the 8th-century master Shantideva, presented the Mahayana path in *A Guide to the Bodhisattva's Way of Life*, beginning with the vow to attain enlightenment and return to the world lifetime after lifetime to save all sentient beings from suffering. In the 8th century, a Nalanda abbot, Shantarakshita, was invited to Tibet by the Buddhist king Trisong Detsen to help him spread the Buddha's teachings in his homeland, and helped to build Samye, the first Tibetan monastery.

The Buddha Shakyamuni in a thangka from 14th-century Tibet. Thangkas are devotional paintings mounted in brocade; the symbols and gestures depicted are meant to represent manifestations of Buddhist principles.

PRESERVATION OF BUDDHISM

As Buddhism spread throughout Asia, the different traditions were influenced by the various cultures. Hinayana became predominant in the south and southeast, while Mahayana was embraced in eastern Asian countries. Both Mahayana and Vajrayana traditions were firmly established in Tibet. The insurgence of Islam in India around the 11th century, followed by the 15th-century Mogul invasion, practically eradicated Buddhism in India. Other Asian countries preserved the Buddhist ways of life, and Tibet, with its high altitude and Himalayan barriers, became a sanctuary in which Buddhism could flourish. A Buddhist civilization formed in Tibet unlike anywhere else in the world and spread into surrounding areas. A remarkable spiritual culture emerged, which produced a rich heritage of art and architecture, visionary Buddhist masters, and a vast body of religious literature. This civilization thrived peacefully for centuries until the Chinese invasion of the 1950s, when many of Tibet's masters were killed and imprisoned, and others were forced to escape into exile. Nepal, the birthplace of the Buddha, and India, where he became enlightened, have become the main places of refuge for Tibetans as they strive to preserve their religion and culture. In this way, Tibetans are helping to bring about a renewal of Buddhism in the place of its birth. They come to Bodhgaya, the holiest site in Buddhism, and with deep devotion, engage in a broad range of spiritual practices at the site of the Buddha's enlightenment.

The 2nd-century Indian master Nagarjuna, *whose Middle Way school of Mahayana Buddhism greatly influenced Tibetan Buddhism, is depicted in this 19th-century thangka from Eastern Tibet.*

The ruins of Nalanda University *in Bihar, above. Founded in the 5th century, Nalanda was the greatest monastic university in India and some its masters had a strong influence on the development of Buddhism in Tibet.*

Bodhgaya, *left, also in Bihar, is the holiest site in Buddhism. It is here that the Buddha attained enlightenment sitting under the "Bodhi Tree" (center). Tibetan monks and nuns participating in the 1997 Nyingma Monlam for World Peace, sit before the great Mahabodhi Stupa, founded by the 3rd century Indian Buddhist king, Ashoka, one of Buddhism's greatest patrons.*

INFLUENCE OF BÖN

Bön is the oldest existing spiritual tradition in Tibet, and its practitioners maintain that aspects of Vajrayana were part of Bön long before the emergence of Buddhism in Tibet in the 8th century. According to Bön practitioners, the religion was founded thousands of years before the life of Shakyamuni Buddha by a prince named Tonpa Shenrab Miwo, whom they believe is an early incarnation of Buddha. Tonpa Shenrab was from Olmo Lung Ring, a mythical city thought to be located in Central Asia, and was sent to the world by Shenlha Okar, the Deity of Compassion, to guide beings out of misery. Pledging his life to spread this doctrine, Tonpa Shenrab eventually arrived in Tibet, where he prophesied that the Dharma would flourish.

BÖN AND BUDDHIST TRADITIONS

Bön and Tibetan Buddhism have a complex relationship of mutual influence. Bön teaches the same message of compassion and wisdom, and has its own extensive canon.

An 18th-century bronze statue from Tibet of Tonpa Shenrab, who is believed by Bön practitioners to have founded Bön thousands of years ago.

A Tibetan woman performing an ancient Bön offering ritual to the mountain spirits at Bön Ri Mountain, Kongpo, Southern Tibet. The shrine is adorned with prayer flags and cotton.

Shenlha Okar ("Shen Deity of White Light"), *one of the four principal Bon deities, is depicted in a 19th-century Nepalese thangka. Arrayed behind him are 250 identical figures representing Enlightened Ones.*

Yeshe Gyaltsen *was a tantric Bön practitioner, or "Bönpo," of the deity Tajka Nebar. He practiced in one cave at Tse Drug Monastery, in eastern Tibet, for over 15 years.*

The most striking difference is the Bön shamanistic connection with nature and its use of ritual in working with natural forces to heal mental and physical imbalances. Tibetan Buddhist culture was heavily influenced by Bön: many aspects of Tibetan medicine and astrology have roots in Bön, as well as the Tibetan Buddhist practices of hanging prayer flags, burning incense, and offering torma (ritual cakes). Mount Kailash, in Tibet, the most sacred mountain for Tibetan Buddhists, is an equally important pilgrimage site for followers of Bön, whose spiritual connection with Mount Kailash reaches back thousands of years. Bön evolved from a more animistic belief system into a monastic tradition that incorporates many aspects of Tibetan Buddhism while maintaining its distinctive character. For example Bön practitioners circumambulate holy places counterclockwise, the opposite direction of Buddhists. Bön and the Nyingma tradition of Tibetan Buddhism both include the teachings of Dzogchen—profound instructions on the ultimate nature of mind that are said to have originated with the primordial Buddha, Samantabhadra.

EVOLUTION OF BUDDHISM IN TIBET

DURING THE REIGN of the Yarlung Empire kings (early 7th to late 9th century), Tibetans were regarded as invincible warriors who ruled large regions of Central Asia. After conquering neighboring Nepal and parts of China, the great Tibetan monarch, Songtsen Gampo (c. 617–50), married a Nepali and then a Chinese princess who were both devout Buddhists. Through their influence, the king converted to Buddhism and built hundreds of temples in his effort to spread the dharma. In the 8th century, the Indian tantric master, Padmasambhava, brought about a massive spiritual conversion, pacifying the country and inspiring the founding of the Nyingma tradition, the first school of Tibetan Buddhism.

Samye Monastery, near Lhasa, *is the first Tibetan Buddhist monastery. It was established in the 8th century by King Trisong Detsen and the Indian masters Padmasambhava and Shantarakshita.*

SCHOOLS OF TIBETAN BUDDHISM

The "second wave" of Buddhism in Tibet was brought about by the Indian scholar, Atisha, in the 11th century. The Buddhist king, Yeshe O, invited Atisha to Tibet and asked him for spiritual instruction that his people could relate to their everyday experience. Atisha summarized the entire Buddhist path, presented moral discipline as the foundation for all spiritual practice, and emphasized the role of the spiritual mentor. The Kadam school that he founded no longer exists, but his teachings profoundly influenced the future of Buddhism in Tibet. Only a few decades after Atisha, two new schools, the Kagyu and Sakya, began to develop. The Kagyu was the first school to maintain their lineage through a line of reincarnate masters, while the Sakya lineage was passed down through a hereditary family line. In the 14th century, a reformation of Buddhism occurred in Tibet with the founding of the Gelug school.

All four schools present the path to complete enlightenment, motivated by compassion for other beings. The present Dalai Lama encourages a nonsectarian approach to Tibetan Buddhism in the spirit of the movement that began in the 19th century known as Rime, which integrated the teachings of all four schools.

A way station for pilgrims in front
of the Potala Palace, in Lhasa, c. 1901; King
Songtsen Gampo founded Lhasa in the
7th century, and built a fortress palace on
the site where the Potala now stands.

FOUNDERS OF TIBETAN BUDDHISM

Padmasambhava is known to Tibetans as Guru Rinpoche, meaning "Precious Teacher." As an expression of the importance of Padmasambhava to all four Tibetan Buddhist traditions, monks of the Kagyu school at Rumtek Monastery in Sikkim, India, carry his image during the Tsechu Festival held in his honor, right. In the 8th century, King Trisong Detsen, a devout Buddhist, wanted to strengthen Buddhism in Tibet. He invited Shantarakshita, the abbot of Nalanda University, for this purpose, but the abbot was unsuccessful due to a series of natural disasters believed to have been invoked by Bön

Monks carry Padmasambhava figure

shamans. Shantarakshita recommended to the king that he ask Padmasambhava to come to Tibet. Padmasambhava's yogic powers overwhelmed those of the Bön priests, and he traveled the country converting local spirits to Buddhism. The king, the abbot, and the yogi founded Samye, the first Tibetan Buddhist monastery. Here, many Buddhist texts were translated from Sanskrit to Tibetan under Padmasambhava's direction. Padmasambhava gave oral transmissions of tantric practices. His consort, Yeshe Tsogyal, a tantric adept, compiled these teachings and concealed them for future adepts to discover.

FOUR TIBETAN BUDDHIST TRADITONS

NYINGMA

THE NYINGMA, OR "ANCIENT TRANSLATION SCHOOL," is the oldest of the four Tibetan schools, and was inspired by the tantric master, Padmasambhava. The Nyingmapas rely on the early translations of Indian Buddhist texts that were overseen by Padmasambhava at Samye monastery in the 8th century, rather than those developed during the second wave of Buddhism in the 11th century.

Followers of Padmasambhava regard him as much more than a historical figure. To them he is an ever-present guide and protector, whom they venerate as much as they do Shakyamuni Buddha. When a Tibetan mother sees her child fall, for example, she says "Guru Rinpoche"—expressing her faith in Padmasambhava's ability to protect her child from harm.

Padmasambhava, founder of the Nyingma tradition, is shown in his "Pure Land" on the Copper Mountain, in this 19th-century Tibetan century thangka painting.

PADMASAMBHAVA'S TEACHINGS

Padmasambhava gave oral teachings on Dzogchen or "Great Perfection," considered by Nyingmapas to be the most profound practice in all of Buddhism. The path of Dzogchen brings about realization of the practioner's original nature, leading to complete enlightenment.

A tradition that Padmasambhava brought from India to Tibet is the transmission of *termas*. These refer to texts and sacred objects that Padmasambhava, together with his consort and main disciple, Yeshe Tsogyal, who was also an accomplished tantric adept, concealed for future generations of practitioners to discover. These have been found over the centuries by realized adepts called *tertons* or "treasure finders" either in the physical environment or through personal revelation. One of these was the *Tibetan Book of the Dead*, which the Dalai Lama has described as one of the most important books our civilization has produced. These teachings were discovered in the 14th century by the terton, Karma Lingpa. The text gives detailed explanations on the process of death and offers guidance to the dying as they experience the transitional states called the *bardos* and on into their next rebirth.

CHOD PRACTICE

Chod is a powerful meditative technique that is primarily practiced by the Nyingma school, but has been adopted by all four schools of Tibetan Buddhism. *Chod* means "to cut," as the aim of this practice is to cut through attachment to the physical body and thus to the sense of self-cherishing and self-identity that lie at the root of all suffering. Chod was developed by the 11th-century female tantric yogi *(yogini)*, Machig Labdron, and is based on the Buddha's Perfection of Wisdom sutras. This practice was performed in cemeteries and cremation grounds. Traditionally, when a Tibetan family loses a loved one, yogis

Yogis of the Nyingma tradition do the practice of Chod, above, with drums (called damarus) *and bells, as they sing verses. Bodhgaya, India, 1997.*

are asked to do chod practice at the place where the ashes are scattered. The chod texts are sung as beautiful verses accompanied by drums and bells, making contact with the deceased person's consciousness and encouraging them to let go of attachment to the physical realm.

KAGYU

KAGYU MEANS "TEACHING LINEAGE," and the teachings of this tradition can be traced back to Tilopa, an 11th-century Indian master. Tilopa's main student was Naropa, abbot of Nalanda university. Although Naropa was a very learned scholar, he came to realize that his understanding of the Dharma was mainly conceptual and that he had not integrated the teachings into his everyday experience. Tilopa put him through twelve years of tests and trials until Naropa was able to access true spiritual realization. Naropa passed the lineage on to Marpa the Translator, a highly realized Tibetan lay practitioner, who then brought these teachings back to Tibet. Perhaps the most famous figure in the Kagyu tradition, however, is the

Monks take part in the procession on the final day of the 49-day funeral for Kalu Rinpoche, above, held at Sonada Monastery near Darjeeling, India, in 1989. Kalu Rinpoche was one of the greatest Buddhist masters of the 20th century.

12th-century yogi Milarepa—Tibet's beloved poet saint. Revered by all Tibetan Buddhist sects, Milarepa's poetry is still a vital part of Tibetan culture today.

ENLIGHTENMENT OF MILAREPA

Milarepa had used his mastery in black magic to cause the death of a number of people whom he believed had cheated his family out of its property. On contemplating what he had done, Milarepa became filled with remorse and looked for a teacher who could guide him on a virtuous path. His search led him to the lay practitioner, Marpa.

Echoing the experiences of his own teacher, Naropa, Marpa set Milarepa a series of arduous physical tasks to purify the negative karma he had created. Then Marpa gave his student the transmissions of his lineage and Milarepa left to become a hermit and internalize what he had learned.

For many years, Milarepa meditated alone in a cave, surviving on nothing but nettles, and devoting himself completely to spiritual practice. Eventually he became fully enlightened, and his poems and songs, which describe the spiritual experience, are revered in all of Tibet's Buddhist traditions. Milarepa's main disciple was the monk, Gampopa, who united the yogic practices of Milarepa within the monastic curriculum that had been established by Atisha. This laid the framework for a tradition that came to place great emphasis on meditation practices as a prerequisite for spiritual development.

KAGYU PRACTICE & LINEAGES

Following Milarepa's example, Kagyu practitioners are known for their intensive retreats and all Kagyu teachers must have completed a retreat of at least three years. Kagyu teachings include yogic practices such as the Six Yogas of Naropa, as well as the practice of *Mahamudra* or "Great Seal"—considered by Kagyupas to be the essence of all Buddha's teachings. Many subschools have developed in the Kagyu tradition, but they are all rooted in these practices.

Mahamudra, which is also a popular practice in the Gelug school, teaches that all phenomena is merely the theater of mind. All conceptual thoughts arise from the *dharmakaya*—the wisdom mind of Buddhahood—in the same way as waves arise from the ocean. Without consciously trying to calm the waves, the meditator focuses on the ocean, and in this way subdues conceptual thought simply through shifting the focus of awareness. Like Dzogchen, the practice of Mahamudra is based on the intimate presence and possibility of spiritual realization. Particularly profound in the context of tantra, this practice is believed to lead to the direct insight into the ultimate nature of reality.

The Kagyu was the first school of Tibetan Buddhism to base a lineage through identifying reincarnations of enlightened teachers. The head of the Karma Kagyu, the main lineage of the Kagyu school, is the Karmapa whom many Tibetans revere as a living Buddha. The present Karmapa is the seventeenth incarnation in this line.

Milarepa, the venerated Kagyu poet yogi, *is shown in this 18th-century Tibetan thangka surrounded by vignettes of his life story.*

On their way *to a ceremony at Kalu Rinpoche's funeral, monks play auspicious music, right, as great masters follow in procession. The lead monk carries a white scarf* (khata), *as an offering to be placed before the body of Kalu Rinpoche in the main shrine.*

SAKYA

THE FIRST SAKYA MONASTERY was constructed in the 11th century by Konchok Gyelpo, who is considered the founder of the Sakya tradition. *Sakya* is Tibetan for "Pale Earth," which refers to the color of the ground where the monastery was established. Konchok Gyelpo was a member of the Khon family, who are said to have descended from celestial beings. The Sakya lineage has continued through family lines up to the present day and the Sakya throne is alternated between two family branches. The present head of the lineage is His Holiness Sakya Trizin (see page 77).

RELATIONSHIP OF SAKYA & MONGOLIA

One of this tradition's greatest figures is the Sakya master, Kunga Gyeltsen, also known as Sakya Pandita or "Scholar of the Sakyas." He was an extraordinary student who became a prolific writer and an accomplished debater, and it is said that he never broke the smallest vow. In 1244, at the age of 62, he cured the Mongol Prince Godan of an illness and became his spiritual advisor. Godan was the grandson of Genghis Khan, and the Tibetan lama's timely intervention averted a Mongolian invasion of Tibet.

Nine years later, Godan's successor, Kublai Khan, invited Sakya Pandita's nephew, Chogyal Pagpa, to Mongolia. He was so impressed with him that he offered the monk the rule of Tibet, and the Sakyas governed there for over a hundred years. This established the "priest-patron" relationship between the Sakya masters and the Mongol rulers in which Tibet exchanged spiritual instruction for military protection.

Monks at the Sakya Center in Rajpur, India, left and top right, under the direction of His Holiness Sakya Trizen, the head of the Sakya order, are taking part in the Vajrakilaya Ceremony, 1997.

LAMDRE TEACHINGS

The unique teaching of the Sakya school is *Lamdre*, which originated with the 9th-century Indian tantric adept, Virupa, and was brought to Tibet in the 11th century by the translator, Drogmi. Virupa, whose ordination name was Dharmapala, was enrolled in a monastic college while he secretly studied tantra. After twelve years, he felt he had made no spiritual progress, but the deity Nairatma appeared to him and informed him that he was actually close to attaining enlightenment. After twelve more years of practice, he attained direct insight into the ultimate nature of reality. Feeling that he had outgrown monastic life, he left the monastery and called himself *Virupa*, meaning "ugly" or "ill-mannered," to denote his transcendence of worldly concerns. He traveled the country performing miraculous deeds; like Padmasambhava, he used yogic powers to impress the populace and convert them to Buddhism.

Lamdre is Tibetan for "path and fruit." The path is the cultivation of method and wisdom, and the fruit is the attainment of buddhahood. These teachings emphasize that enlightened and unenlightened existence (*nirvana* and *samsara*) only appear to us as one or the other, due to our own perceptions. Nirvana cannot be attained by rejecting samsara because the mind is the foundation of both. Through meditation, Lamdre practitioners learn to realize that samsara exists when the mind is obscured by ignorance and other afflictions. Nirvana is when these obscurations have been overcome. Up until the 11th century, the Lamdre teachings remained a closely guarded oral tradition, and even today, students take an oath of secrecy when they receive these teachings. Like the Gelug school, the Sakya order emphasizes scholarly training and monasteries offer degrees in Buddhist study.

The great master Sakya Pandita, *shown on the left of this 16th-century Tibetan thangka, was the first Tibetan spiritual advisors to the Mongol rulers. His nephew, Chogyal Pagpa (seated at right), cemented this relationship as advisor to Kublai Khan.*

GELUG

TRANSLATED FROM TIBETAN as "Followers of the Virtuous Path," Gelug was established in the 14th century by Tsongkhapa, widely regarded as one of Tibet's greatest Buddhist masters. Tsongkhapa, or "Je Rinpoche," as he is affectionately known among Tibetans, was a child prodigy who excelled in everything he was taught. He took the vows of a lay Buddhist when he was only three years of age, and the vows of a novice monk when he was seven. He traveled around the country and received teachings with over one hundred eminent masters from all lineages of Tibetan Buddhism. He developed a wide following and taught frequently. He had a universal and eclectic approach to the Dharma and sometimes even tutored his own teachers. He was a prolific writer, and went on to compose eighteen volumes of Buddhist doctrine, the most influential being The Great Exposition of the Stages of the Path to Enlightenment, which was based on the teachings of Atisha. Besides being a scholar, however, Tsongkhapa was also an accomplished yogi who engaged in extensive meditation retreats.

*A **Tibetan thangka** from the 16th century, portrays Tsongkhapa, founder of the Gelug school, flanked by his two students, Gyaltsab (left) and Khedrup (right). The Buddha Shakyamuni is at the top center, with two bodhisattvas and three rows of lineage gurus.*

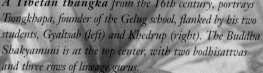

ORDINATION

Monks receive instruction from His Holiness the Dalai Lama during their full ordination ceremony held at his residence in Dharamsala, India. The

first monastic community was established by the Buddha. He elucidated the rules of monastic life, which were later preserved in the texts of the *vinaya,* meaning "discipline." Little has changed since this time. The Buddha's code of conduct for ordained men and women is still followed

The Dalai Lama giving ordination, 1997

today, from guidelines for running a monastery, down to the dimensions of a monk's room. It is said that wherever there is a monk or nun

observing the vows of full ordination, the Buddha himself is present. There are different levels of ordination, each requiring a greater degree of

mindfulness and discipline. A *getsul,* or novice monk, has thirty-six vows, whereas a *gelong* or fully ordained monk has 253 vows. A gelong candidate should have undergone several years of practice and study under the guidance of a qualified teacher and be at least twenty years old. The lineage for

fully ordained nuns was not transmitted in Tibet, so a Tibetan Buddhist nun seeking full ordination must receive it through other Buddhist traditions.

FOUNDATIONS OF GELUG

Tsongkhapa dedicated himself to reforming Tibetan Buddhism, which he felt had lost some of its authenticity and purity, and particularly emphasized the need for monks and nuns to follow the *vinaya,* the monastic code of ethical conduct that the Buddha had taught. He founded Ganden Monastery, one of the three great Gelug monastic universities, the others being Drepung and Sera. The Gelug school presents the path to enlightenment as a series of gradual steps in a system called *Lamrim* or "Stages of the Path," and emphasizes the "three principle aspects of the path"—renunciation of worldly attachments, the altruistic determination to achieve enlightenment for others, and a correct understanding of the nature of reality. In the 16th century, the Mongol chieftain Altan Khan conferred the title of Dalai Lama on Sonam Gyatso, the second reincarnation of one of Tsongkhapa's main disciples. The authority of the Gelug school was later consolidated when the Fifth Dalai Lama founded the first Tibetan government. All subsequent Dalai Lamas have belonged to the Gelug school, but also serve as the supreme head of all four schools of Tibetan Buddhism. The Gelug school emphasizes scholarship as an essential foundation for meditative practice within a monastic lifestyle. Many Gelug monastics study for their geshe degree, a doctorate of Buddhist philosophy, which was instituted by the Thirteenth Dalai Lama. Another of Tsongkhapa's disciples, Gyaltsab, became the first Ganden Tripa or "throne holder" of Ganden. Although the Dalai Lamas are temporal and spiritual leaders of Tibet, it is the Ganden Tripa who is the actual head of the Gelug school. To hold this title, a monk must be a *geshe lharampa,* the highest geshe level, but does not have to be a reincarnate lama. Tibetan parents use the Ganden Tripa as an example to their children of how almost anyone, no matter what their background, can reach one of the most esteemed positions in Tibetan society.

Monks from Ganden Shartse monastery *in Mundgod, south India, came to Dharamsala to receive their full ordination from His Holiness the Dalai Lama, in the temple within his residence, called the Phodang, 1997. For these monks, seen listening intently to the Dalai Lama's instructions, it is one of the most important moments of their lives.*

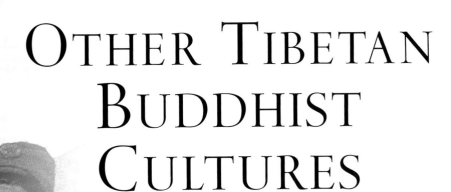

OTHER TIBETAN BUDDHIST CULTURES

གཞན་ཡང་བོད་ཀྱི་ནང་པའི་རིག་གཞུང་།

TIBETAN BUDDHISM HAS BEEN PRACTICED for centuries in the lands bordering Tibet. From as early as the 8th century, there was a steady flow of Tibetan masters into the Himalayan kingdoms and north into Mongolia and parts of Siberia. At the same time, monks from these areas came to study Buddhism in Tibet and returned to influence their own cultures. Tibetan monasteries can also be found in parts of China far from Tibet. The migrations and trading activities of Tibetan nomads and merchants, along with the influence of Buddhist monarchs, all contributed to the spread of Tibetan Buddhism into the surrounding regions. The remoteness of these areas, combined with the fact that a number of them have only recently opened their borders to foreign visitors, have made them precious refuges for Tibetan Buddhist culture. Now that Tibetan Buddhism is threatened in its homeland, these areas have become vital to the survival of this profound spiritual tradition.

People of the Zanskar valley of Ladakh came to see His Holiness the Dalai Lama, who made a rare visit there to give teachings in 1997. Ladakh, located on the Tibetan plateau, is a sanctuary of Tibetan Buddhist culture.

INDIA

THERE ARE SEVERAL AREAS in India where Tibetan Buddhism has been continuously sustained from antiquity to the present day. They include Ladakh and Zanskar in the northwest and Sikkim in the northeast—former Buddhist kingdoms that were annexed by India in the mid-20th century—and in part of the northwestern state of Himachal Pradesh.

LADAKH & ZANSKAR

It is believed that Buddhism reached Ladakh as long ago as the 3rd century BC, via missionaries sent by the venerated Indian Buddhist king, Ashoka. However, Buddhism was not firmly established in this mountainous region until the 10th century, when Ladakh and Zanskar became sanctuaries for Tibetan Buddhism during a time of great persecution of Buddhism in Tibet. The famed 11th-century Tibetan translator, Lochen Rinchen Zangpo, founded many chortens and temples in the area. Located at the crossroads of the Himalayas and Central Asia, the inhabitable regions of Ladakh and Zanskar have average altitudes of 11,000 feet (3,300 m), and their rugged and remote landscapes have been compared to the surface of the moon.

Geographically part of the Tibetan plateau, these areas have more cultural, historical, linguistic, and ancestral ties with Tibet than with India. The Ladakhi and Zanskari people mainly practice Tibetan Buddhism, and speak Tibetan dialects. There are many important monasteries here that contain extraordinary, ancient Buddhist paintings and sculptures, and support an active monastic community dedicated to preserving the purity of Tibetan Buddhist practice. Many people from this region are descended from the intermarriage of ethnic Tibetans and Indo-European tribes. One of these remaining tribes are the Dards or Dardshin, a small ethnic group in areas of Kashmir bordering Ladakh. The Dardshin incorporate Tibetan Buddhism into their religious practice. With an extreme climate and geographical isolation (Zanskar is inaccessible nine months a year), Ladakhis and Zanskaris have been able to preserve the integrity of their cultural traditions and maintain deep spiritual faith over the centuries.

SIKKIM

The Buddhist master, Padmasambhava, described Sikkim as being the holiest of all the lands he had visited. The Bhutias, one of the three main ethnic groups, settled here in the 14th century and are of Tibetan origin. The capital city of Gangtok even hosts an institute of Tibetan studies.

The original buildings of Rumtek Monastery, constructed for the 16th Karmapa after he fled Tibet, as seen from a vantage point at the expanded present-day Rumtek monastery, near Gangtok, Sikkim, 1997.

A Zanskari woman, left, wearing a traditional headdress studded with turquoise, carrying a prayer wheel.

People of the ethnic group known as Dards, or Dardshin, listen to a talk given by the Dalai Lama, near the town of Cargil, in Kashmir, 1997.

Today, there are about sixty Tibetan Buddhist monasteries in Sikkim. One of the oldest is the 17th-century Nyingma monastery of Pemagyantse, but perhaps the most famous is Rumtek, which was founded in the 1960s with the help of the Sikkimese royal family. Rumtek became the seat of the sixteenth Karmapa after he fled from Tibet; the head of the Karma Kagyu tradition, the Karmapa is one of the most revered Tibetan Buddhist masters. The establishment of this monastery was vital in conserving the teaching traditions and lineage of this school.

HIMACHAL PRADESH

Several areas in the Indian state of Himachal Pradesh are home to hill tribes that have practiced Tibetan Buddhism for centuries, including the Kinnaur, Lahaul-Spiti, Chamba, and the Kullu Valley. The people of Spiti are mostly Buddhist, as well as the people of Upper Kinnaur, which is close to Tibet. Kardang Monastery in Lahaul is almost 1,000 years old, while Kyi and Tabo monasteries in the Spiti valley were both founded around the 11th century. No one knows why, but along the sides of the Sutlej River, which flows from Mount Kailash through Kinnaur to Pakastan, the monasteries on the right bank facing northwest are Gelug, and those on the other side are Drukpa Kagyu.

Two Kinnauri women from Himachal Pradesh are with a group of Tibetan monks who are seen chanting sacred texts at Bodhgaya in 1997.

The Kinnauris and several other Himachal hill tribes have been practicing Tibetan Buddhism for many centuries.

NEPAL

Tucked between the borders of India to the south, west, and east, and Tibet to the North, Nepal is home to some of the holiest sites in Buddhism. Lumbini, just north of the Indian border, is the birthplace of Shakyamuni Buddha. Buddhists come from many countries to go on pilgrimage in Lumbini, and the Sakya tradition of Tibetan Buddhism holds its annual Monlam ceremonies there. The great Bodhnath Stupa in Kathmandu is deeply sacred for Vajrayana Buddhists, because it is believed to contain relics of the previous Buddha,

The Great Stupa (called Chorten Chempo *by Tibetans), above, is one of the world's largest stupas, measuring 131 feet (40 m) in both height and diameter. It was erected during the reign of King Mana Dev in the 5th century. Eyes are painted on all four sides of the spire bases, a Nepali feature referring to the "all-seeing eyes" of the Buddha.*

Bodhnath is adorned with hundreds of prayer flags. These Buddhist pilgrims, photographed in 1989, are among the thousands who make pilgrimages every year to the Great Stupa.*

Kasyapa. The village of Boudha, next to Bodhnath Stupa, and the nearby area around Swayumbu—which has an important but smaller stupa—is mostly populated with Tibetan refugees and Nepali Buddhists. Some of Tibet's greatest Buddhist masters have built monasteries there. Every day, thousands of Tibetans and Nepalis circumambulate around Bodhanath Stupa, reciting mantras and counting prayer beads as they walk briskly.

BUDDHISM IN NEPAL

Hinduism is the state religion of Nepal, although many Nepalis practice both Buddhism and Hinduism, and there are a number of ethnic groups that are primarily Buddhist. These groups include the Mananges and Tamangs,

Members of the Tamang hill tribe who have settled in Kathmandu, circumambulate around Bodhanath Stupa, 1997. The Tamangs are one of a number of Nepali ethnic groups who are said to be descendants of people who migrated from Tibet centuries before.

descendants of people who migrated from Tibet centuries earlier. The Tamangs live in many areas along the Indian border and in India as well, especially around Darjeeling. The Sherpas, famous for their mountaineering skills, originally arrived in Nepal from Kham in Eastern Tibet, and have been able to successfully maintain their Tibetan Buddhist culture in remote mountain areas.

MUSTANG

Far from Kathmandu on the border of Tibet is the former kingdom of Mustang, which until recently, was inaccessible to foreigners. Mustang has some of the oldest monasteries in the Himalayas and their precious Tibetan Buddhist wall paintings are currently undergoing extensive restoration by a team of international experts. The Lhopas and Thakalis are the main ethnic groups of Mustang. When China invaded Tibet in the 1950s, Mustang requested that it be incorporated into the country of Nepal. In doing so, Mustang was able to protect its Tibetan culture and monasteries.

The Nepalese hill tribe, the Tamangs, are Buddhists, and these parents sent their son to live in a Tibetan monastery in Darjeeling, India, left, 1989.

On the following pages, Tamangs and Tibetans light candles as spiritual offerings at Bodhnath Stupa, 1997.

BHUTAN

THE HIMALAYAN KINGDOM OF BHUTAN—Druk Yul, "Land of the Thunder Dragon," as the people of Bhutan call their country—is the only remaining nation where Vajrayana Buddhism is practiced as a state religion. Located to the southeast of the Tibetan plateau, Bhutan is a mountainous and deeply forested country, in which Buddhism is the very fabric of social, political, and cultural life. The Buddhist king, Jigme Singye Wangchuk, has made a great effort to keep the culture intact, including rigorously protecting the natural environment, requiring Bhutanese to wear traditional dress, and severely restricting tourism. Monasteries are partially supported by the government and foreigners are not allowed inside them. The king has been quoted as saying:

This 1974 photo by acclaimed photographer Ernst Haas shows dancers leaping into the air during coronation festivities for King Wangchuk, in Tashichho Dzong, the seat of the Bhutanese royal government in Thimpu.

These Bhutanese families *came to India in 1997 to attend the Kalachakra Initiation given by His Holiness the Dalai Lama, and to go on pilgrimage to Bodhgaya in the state of Bihar.*

"I am less interested in the gross national product, than I am in the gross national happiness." Older Tibetans who have been to Bhutan say that the country is like Tibet before the Chinese invasion.

ORIGINS OF BUDDHISM IN BHUTAN

Two of the country's most important temples—Kyichu Lhakhang and Jampe Lhakhang—were said to have been built by the 7th-century Tibetan king, Songtsen Gampo, who initially brought Tibetan Buddhism to Bhutan. According to legend, he went to Bhutan to defeat a giant demoness who was impeding the spread of Buddhism. To stop her, the king constructed 108 temples on the demoness's joints in a single day. The most important figure in the development of Buddhism in Bhutan was the 8th-century Indian tantric master Padmasambhava, who is believed to have made his trip from Tibet to Bhutan on the back of a flying tigress, landing in a cave on the side of a cliff and entering retreat there. In the 17th century, a monastery was built on the cliff, named Takstang Lhakang, or "Tiger's Nest." It is one of the most sacred sites in Bhutan.

Tiger's Nest Monastery, *in Bhutan, left, clings precariously to the mountainside. The tulku (reincarnation) of Padmasambhava, is said to reside at the monastery.*

A Bhutanese woman, *right, who journeyed to Sonada Monastery near Darjeeling, India, to attend the funeral of Kalu Rinpoche in 1989.*

MONGOLIA

MONGOLIA AND TIBET have maintained a close political and spiritual alliance since the 13th century, when Tibetan Buddhism took root in Mongolia. One of the factors that may have eased the way to Mongolia's conversion to Tibetan Buddhism was the similarity of their indigenous religious beliefs. Another factor was the invasion of Tibet by Godan Khan in 1240 and the subsequent influence wielded by Phagba, a Tibetan Buddhist master who succeeded his uncle, Sakya Pandita (patriarch of the Sakya sect) to the Mongol Court in 1253. Phagba became Kublai Khan's spiritual advisor and introduced others in the Mongolian ruling class to Tibetan Buddhism. Three centuries later, in 1578, Altan Khan, the Mongolian ruler, conferred the title of Dalai Lama ("Ocean of Wisdom") on his Tibetan teacher, Sonam Gyatso. With the construction of the great monastic university, Erdeni Dzu, from the stones of Karakorum, the former capital of the Mongol empire, Mongolia experienced a spiritual and cultural renaissance. Most Monglians regard the Dalai Lama as their spiritual leader, although they also revere the reincarnate lineage of the Khalkha Jetsun Dampas, the title bestowed on a descendent of Genghis Khan by the Fifth Dalai Lama.

Erdeni Dzu Monastery, central Republic of Mongolia. This celebrated monastery was built in 1586, near Karakatorum, an ancient Mongol city.

Mongolians attend a ceremony at Ganden Monastery, Ulaanbaatar, Mongolia. ca. 1984. Built in 1840, it is the most important monastery in Mongolia—and the only one to survive the Communist purges of the 1930s.

MODERN MONGOLIA

By the turn of the 20th century, Tibetan Buddhism had become an integral part of Mongolian culture, with one-third of the male population ordained as monks. But in the 1930s, Mongolia fell under Soviet control and Buddhism was almost obliterated. Seventeen thousand monks perished in Siberian labor camps, and only a handful of monasteries survived. Since the collapse of Communism, Mongolians have been struggling to restore their Buddhist heritage, often finding themselves in competition with Western Christian missionaries. However, Buddhist knowledge remains mostly in the hands of the elderly, so Mongolian students have been studying at Tibetan monasteries in India and returning to Mongolia to reeducate the young.

RUSSIA

IN THE EARLY 17TH CENTURY, Tibetan Buddhism spread north from Mongolia to the eastern shores of Lake Baikal, in southern Siberia, Russia. Here it became established in a mountainous area called Buryatia, which had been part of the Mongolian empire since the 13th century. In 1741, Russian Empress Elizabeth (the daughter of Peter the Great and Catherine I) issued a decree that officially incorporated Buryatia into Russia. (The Buryats were and still are the largest Buddhist population in Russia.) In the latter half of the 17th century, Buddhism emerged as the dominant religion in Kalmykia, whose people originally migrated from China to the lower reaches of the Volga, and in Tuva, which shares borders with Mongolia and Buryatia. In pre-revolutionary Russia, where orthodox Christianity was the predominant religion, Buddhists were tolerated by Tsarist authorities and allowed to build temples and monasteries, mainly in Central Asia and Siberia. By 1846, 34 *datsans* (Buddhist monasteries) had been built in Buryatia, and in order to consolidate

Russia's diplomatic ties with the Dalai Lama's government in Tibet, a Buddhist temple was built in the capital, St. Petersburg, in 1915. This receptive atmosphere, however, lasted for only a few more years.

The Ven. Khambo Lama Tsybykzhapov, from Siberia, was a delegate to the World Fellowship of Buddhists conference in southern California in 1988.

REPRESSION AND REBIRTH

By the late 1920s, Soviet leader Joseph Stalin (1879–1953) had issued anti-religious laws that resulted in the repression of Buddhism and the destruction of almost every monastery and temple in the U.S.S.R. Hundreds, if not thousands, of Buddhists were executed or deported to Stalin's notorious gulags. But pockets of religious belief remained alive, particularly in the remote areas of Russia where Buddhism first took hold—in Buryatia, Tuva, and Kalmykia. Since the advent of *perestroika* in the late 1980s and the collapse of the Soviet Union in 1991, there has been a tremendous revival of Buddhism all over Russia: Monasteries and temples have been reopened or rebuilt; young lamas are being trained; and Buddhist spiritual life has resumed.

Ivolginsk Datsan, Russia's largest Buddhist monastery, near Ulan Ude, the capital of Buryatia, was rebuilt in 1946, after decades of Communist repression and neglect.

TIBETAN DIASPORA

ཉེས་འཁྲུར་བཞིང་མེ།

RATHER THAN LIVE under the repressive regime of the Chinese communist government, many thousands of Tibetan refugees have fled into exile, and large numbers continue to make the perilous trek across the high Himalayan passes from Tibet. They arrive with few personal possessions and face formidable challenges of economic survival as well as those of adapting to a different culture and climate. Tibetans traditionally maintain very close family units, but the Chinese occupation and the resultant diaspora of refugees have torn many families apart. Over ninety percent of Tibetan refugees live in settlements on government-donated land in India and Nepal, and over one hundred monasteries have been reestablished. The Tibetan Government-in-Exile has done a remarkable job of preserving the integrity of Tibetan life. Although rehabilitation has been largely successful, the recent dramatic increase of refugees from Tibet has created a serious burden on the existing refugee communities. There are currently 140,000 Tibetan people living in exile today.

Tibetan refugees in Himachal Pradesh, India, in 1997, gather at a local school to recite a mantra for several hours a day over a few weeks. Prayer beads are used to count how many times they recite the mantra and prayer wheels are turned at the same time. The collective recitation of the mantra is added up to reach the goal set by a Buddhist master.

INVASION & PERSECUTION

BUDDHISM FORMS the very essence of Tibetan civilization, and defines Tibetans both as a people and a nation. Following its invasion of Tibet in the 1950s, China embarked on a brutal campaign of religious repression to replace Buddhism with Communism, and consolidate its control of the country. In the two decades that followed, over 6,000 Tibetan Buddhist monasteries were destroyed. Of the 500,000 Tibetan monks and nuns in the monastic community, over 110,000 were tortured and put to death, and 250,000 were forcibly disrobed in a brutal campaign that the Dalai Lama has described as a "Buddhist holocaust." Including laypeople, over 1.2 million Tibetans have been killed. In the 1980s, the Chinese lifted some restrictions on religion in the hope of winning the support of the Tibetan people. However, they were unprepared for how vigorously Tibetans renewed their spiritual activities. During the ensuing

In one of the first photographs of the Chinese invasion of Tibet, soldiers from the Peoples Liberation Army (PLA) are shown building a bridge across one of Tibet's rivers while an Army vehicle and troops are transported across in rubber rafts, 1950.

TIBET'S WARRIOR NUN

Ani Pachen's father was an important chieftain in Eastern Tibet. When he died in 1958, Ani Pachen, an ordained nun, assumed leadership of the district. Ani Pachen, which means "warrior nun" in Tibetan, led 700 men and women on horseback against the invading Chinese army. After her capture in 1960, she spent the next 21 years in Chinese prisons, where she secretly continued her spiritual practices and used the punishment of solitary confinement to engage in meditation retreats. Her unshakable faith enabled her to endure horrific torture and maintain compassion for those who inflicted it.

During her ordeal, she never renounced her devotion to His Holiness the Dalai Lama or her belief in a free Tibet. Ani Pachen was released in 1981, and facing rearrest, she escaped over the Himalayas to India seven years later. She remained a tireless activist for the Tibetan cause until her death in 2002, and never lost hope for the future of her country and people. "If they couldn't break one old woman like me," she is quoted as saying, "how can they break the spirit of Tibet?"

Ani Pachen

crackdown that began in the 1990s, hundreds of monks and nuns were arrested, and tens of thousands were expelled from monastic institutions for refusing to denounce the Dalai Lama and accept Tibet as part of China. Up to one thousand still linger in prison where torture is commonplace. This current campaign of religious repression in Tibet is ongoing and has created a climate of fear that the Dalai Lama has compared to the dark days of the Cultural Revolution.

BUDDHISM IN TIBET TODAY

Buddhism in today's Tibet is a pale shadow of its former self. Many monasteries have been relegated to the role of museums, with the monks and nuns reduced to acting as caretakers and curiosities for the tourist industry. Chinese authorities have also relaxed

A Tibetan woman flees Tibet in 1950, carrying her possessions on her back as she heads over the Himalayas to India.

restrictions on certain external expressions of religious practice, such as circumambulating sacred sites, making prostrations, making offerings, turning prayer wheels, and putting up prayer flags, but the study of the Buddha's teachings remains severely restricted. As the Dalai Lama has stated: "The so-called religious freedom in Tibet today amounts to permitting our people to worship and practice religion in a merely ritualistic and devotional way. . . . Buddhism, thus, is being reduced to blind faith which is exactly how the Communist Chinese view and define religion." In some remote regions, however, Buddhist practice has maintained its original integrity. With the inspiration of Tibetan Buddhist masters outside Tibet and help from foreign supporters, a number of monasteries are being rebuilt and funds are being sent to support the monks and nuns. Despite enormous obstacles, Tibetans are trying to save their traditional way of life in their homeland.

On March 10, 1959, now known as Tibetan National Uprising Day, huge demonstrations in Lhasa were brutally suppressed by the PLA. At left, members of the resistance are marched out of the Potala Palace by the PLA, May 9, 1959.

TIBETAN REFUGEE COMMUNITY
STRUGGLE FOR SURVIVAL

ALMOST HALF OF ALL TIBETAN refugees today are under twenty-five, either seeking job opportunities denied them in their homeland or pursuing an education. Most of the refugees from Tibet are monks and nuns fleeing religious persecution and many are former prisoners of conscience in need of medical care. Coping with the flood of new arrivals, whose numbers increase every year, has become one of the most pressing issues confronting the Tibetan Government-in-Exile. Stretched to the limit of their generosity, host governments in India and Nepal have have not allocated any new land for resettlement. In addition, foreign NGOs (non-governmental organizations) have reduced their assistance in recent years, viewing the Tibetan exile community as a success story. There is no longer room in the already overcrowded settlements, and many Tibetan refugees continue to live in camps under extremely poor conditions.

His Holiness the Dalai Lama regularly gives public audiences at his residence for newly arrived Tibetan refugees. To be able to receive his blessings, after having lived their whole lives cut off from him, is a profoundly moving experience for refugees. Dharamsala, India 1997.

A Tibetan woman and her daughter camp in Kalimpong, West Bengal, India, after fleeing over the Himalyas, 1951.

A COMMUNITY AT RISK

Apart from the challenges of cultural and economic survival, Tibetans face many health issues that were previously rare in their homeland. The Tibetan diet, developed for the cooler temperatures of the Himalayan plateau, is unsuitable for a subtropical climate, and diseases such as diabetes are occurring at an epidemic rate. Tuberculosis, formerly almost unheard of among Tibetans, has also become a serious health problem in refugee communities. Well over 10,000 Tibetans from the first wave of refugees have yet to be resettled, and the influx of new refugees since 1986 has already increased the existing refugee population by over ten percent. Without continuing aid and assistance, the Tibetan refugee community will not be able to respond to the needs of those who still seek freedom in exile.

TIBETAN WEAVING PROJECTS

An international effort to help support the economic and cultural life of the Tibetan community in exile has resulted in the formation of various large-scale weaving projects in Nepal and India. One of the oldest and most successful of these, The Cultural Survival Tibetan Weaving Project, established in 1990, has also built and sponsored shipments of food and books to schools, and has provided an education, and room and board to over 70 Tibetan refugee students in Nepal. In the various Tibetan settlements, carpet weaving is the main way that refugees can earn a living while preserving an important cultural tradition. The Tibetan exile government, and many of the monasteries, have established handicraft centers in India and Nepal, where master weavers from Tibet are passing their skills on to younger Tibetans. Income from the sale of beautiful, handwoven wool rugs, treasured for their traditional designs by Tibetans and foreigners alike, helps to support the exile government's social programs and monasteries. These centers also make and sell a broad variety of traditional crafts. In the photo, a little boy is given day care while his grandmother works at a loom.

A Tibetan woman weaving in Leh, Ladakh, India, 1997.

Dharamsala, the seat of the Tibetan Government-in-Exile, has welcomed more Tibetan refugees than any other city. In the 1950s, few of Tibet's neighbors were willing to open their doors to refugees for fear of antagonizing China. India, however, offered them asylum in Dharamsala. The city is also the home of His Holiness the 14th Dalai Lama.

SCHOOLS & ORPHANAGES

A LARGE NUMBER OF THE NEW REFUGEES coming into exile from Tibet are children and teenagers. Many of the younger children are sent by their parents to neighboring countries such as India in order to get a Tibetan education in a less repressive environment. Teenagers and young adults seek educational opportunities as well, while looking for job training and employment. The Tibetan Government-in-Exile has mandated that all Tibetan refugee children must attend school, and almost half of the resources of the Tibetan refugee community is spent on education. As a result, there is almost universal literacy among young Tibetan refugees. This success has been largely due to the accomplishments of the Central Tibetan Schools Administration, which is funded by the government of India. The Tibetan Homes Foundation and the Tibetan Children's Village (TCV) have also made enormous contributions to the educational, cultural, and personal needs of refugee children, particularly those who have been orphaned or separated from their families.

ADVOCATES FOR TIBETAN CHILDREN

JETSUN PEMA

Founded in 1959, the Tibetan Children's Village (TCV) is run by Jetsun Pema, the Dalai Lama's sister. TCV cares for 15,000 children throughout India in numerous villages, residential and day schools, daycare and vocational centers, farm projects, and hostels. Great care is taken to provide educational and job training, as well as a grounding in Tibetan traditions and language. In 1999, Mrs. Pema wrote her life story; she received the "Woman of Courage" award in 2002.

RINCHEN DOLMA TARING

The Tibetan Homes Foundation, a boarding school for Tibetan refugee orphans, was founded in 1962 by Rinchen Dolma Taring (affectionately known as "Taring Amala") and her husband, Jigme Taring. In July 2002, at the age of 92, she died in Rajpur, India, after four decades of impassioned dedication to the education and welfare of Tibetan children. She published a memoir in 1987. See pages 152–155 for commentary by both Jetsun Pema and Taring Amala.

Traditional music and dance are a vital part of the school curriculum and an important means of preserving Tibetan culture in exile. Here a group of children play traditional instruments, Tibetan Children's Village, Leh, Ladakh, 1997.

KEEPING TIBETAN VALUES ALIVE

Many of the schools that are entrusted with the education of Tibetan children are residential because one-third of the children are orphans or have been separated from their families. Modeling the communal intimacy and kinship of Tibetan family life, the schools house children in tight-knit groups, where, under the supervision of foster parents, the children play, eat, study, and pray together. These educational institutions also manage a number of youth hostels and vocational training centers that prepare young Tibetans to compete as professionals in the technological arena. Other programs are aimed at maintaining the integrity of traditional occupations, such as farming and animal husbandry. In Ladakh, for example, a new generation of Tibetans are learning how best to preserve and develop their nomadic way of life.

The Tibetan Government-in-Exile provides daycare programs for children whose parents are working in refugee handicraft centers. These children are taking a nap at a daycare center near Kathmandu, Nepal, 1997.

CARING FOR THE ELDERLY

EVERY YEAR, THERE ARE FEWER Tibetans who remember an independent Tibet.
Of the first generation of exiles, many have died and the rest have now grown old.
Almost 15,000 Tibetans in the refugee community are over sixty—about 12 percent of
the entire refugee population. Although almost half of the elderly exile community is
self-sufficient, many are now in need of assistance. In Tibetan society, the concept
of "old people's homes" was unheard of because the elderly are considered an integral
and respected part of the family. In exile, however, the structure of the traditional
family has changed. Now, without support from relatives who may be either too
poor themselves to be of help, or who were left behind in Tibet, many elders
are on their own at a particularly vulnerable time of life. There are at least two
good alternatives, however, to homelessness and poverty: elders' homes in
refugee settlements and monasteries.

An older Tibetan woman
prepares yarn for weaving in Leh,
Ladakh, India, 1997.

*News **that is important*** *to the Tibetan community is posted on a wall near the Dalai Lama's residence in Dharamsala, which Tibetans refer to as his palace. As Tibetans circumambulate around the palace, they pass by this wall and stop to read the latest bulletins.*

*At **home in a refugee settlement*** *in Himachal Pradesh, India, 1997, two friends enjoy each other's company while one of their relatives prepares a meal in the kitchen.*

HOUSING OPTIONS FOR ELDERS

One of the first Tibetan elders' homes was constructed in 1971 in Mundgod, at a refugee settlement in southern India. A second was built in 1992. Like many others of its kind, each of the facilities in Mundgod has a common prayer hall where the residents gather every morning for a *puja* (an offering). For older Tibetans, spiritual practice is a priority, and they spend much of their time reciting prayers and circumambulating the temples and stupas nearby. The elders at Mundgod enjoy various activities such as picnics and pilgrimages, and have access to common facilities. A few monasteries, such as Palyul Namdroling in Bylakuppe, a settlement near the

southern Indian city of Mysore, also offer a place for elderly Tibetans to live and concentrate on their spiritual life. However, much of the housing that is currently available to older people is overcrowded and underfunded, and foreign support for the residents, through individual sponsorship, is sorely needed.

*A **group of Tibetan elders*** *who live in the old age home at Palyul Namdroling Nyingmapa Monastery in Bylakuppe, southern India, are joined by others from the large refugee settlement there, 1997. Each person in the group turns a prayer wheel as they recite mantras.*

Each year on March 10, *Tibetans in exile gather to protest in refugee settlements to raise awareness about conditions in Tibet; above and right, protests in Mundgod, South India, 1997.*

PROTESTS

OVER THE PAST FIFTY YEARS, Tibetans have engaged in many kinds of protests against the occupation, almost all of a nonviolent nature. The most famous uprising occurred in Tibet's capital, Lhasa, on March 10, 1959—a date that holds deep significance for the Tibetan people. The Chinese authorities had invited the Dalai Lama to a dance performance, stating that he should come without an escort. Word of this spread quickly around the city, and soon thousands of people had surrounded the Norbulingka, the Dalai Lama's summer residence, intent on protecting their leader from what was thought to be a plot to abduct or assassinate him. The Chinese ordered the crowd to disperse, but it continued to grow, and two days later 5,000 Tibetan women took to the streets in protest. On March 17, knowing that his capture would only result in further violence, the young Dalai Lama made the decision to leave Tibet, and using the crowd for cover, he made his escape disguised as a Tibetan soldier. Chinese soldiers shelled the city and the Norbulingka for three days, believing that he was still inside. Thousands of men, women, and children who had camped outside the Norbulingka were slaughtered, and many more Tibetans in Central Tibet were killed during this period. Over the next few months, over 80,000 Tibetans followed the Dalai Lama into exile.

THE FIGHT FOR HUMAN RIGHTS

March 10 is commemorated with protests by the Tibetan people as a way of remembering these events and raising awareness in their cause for freedom and human rights in Tibet. In Europe and America, they are often joined by Western supporters. It has become a tradition for the Dalai Lama to make a statement on this date, which is posted on the exiled Tibetan government's website and gives hope and encouragement to Tibetans around the world. Many protests occurred in Tibet in the 1980s. These demonstrations were brutally repressed and thousands of Tibetans were arrested and imprisoned without trial. Torture is commonplace. The majority of political prisoners are monks and nuns under thirty and many are only teenagers. The reincarnation of the Panchen Lama, the second highest-ranking Tibetan spiritual leader, was arrested by the Chinese in 1995 when he was only six years old, and his whereabouts are still unknown.

HIS HOLINESS THE DALAI LAMA

ༀ་གོང་ས་སྐྱབས་མགོན་ཏུ་ལའི་བླ་མ་མཆོག

FOR ALMOST SIX CENTURIES, the Dalai Lamas were the primary religious authorities of Tibet, as well as spiritual guides to powerful Mongol rulers and Chinese emperors. All of the Dalai Lamas are regarded as reincarnations of Avalokiteshvara, the Buddha of Compassion. They are also all distinct individuals who have made important contributions to history. The Fifth Dalai Lama formed Tibet's first national government in the 17th century and became the secular as well as the spiritual head of a unified nation. The lineage of the Dalai Lamas ruled Tibet for the next three hundred years— overseeing a remarkable society in which spiritual development was more valued than material progress and where moral force took precedence over military power. It is difficult to adequately describe the devotion that Tibetans feel for the Dalai Lama. When he escaped into exile in 1959, one Tibetan remarked, "It was as if the sun had left us." It is a source of great pride for the Tibetan people that His Holiness the Dalai Lama has since become one of the most beloved and revered spiritual leaders in the world.

His Holiness the Dalai Lama gave teachings in New York City in 1999, as well as a public talk in Central Park. The events were hosted by The Tibet Center under the direction of Reverend Khyongla Rato Rinpoche, and by Richard Gere.

SACRED LEGACY

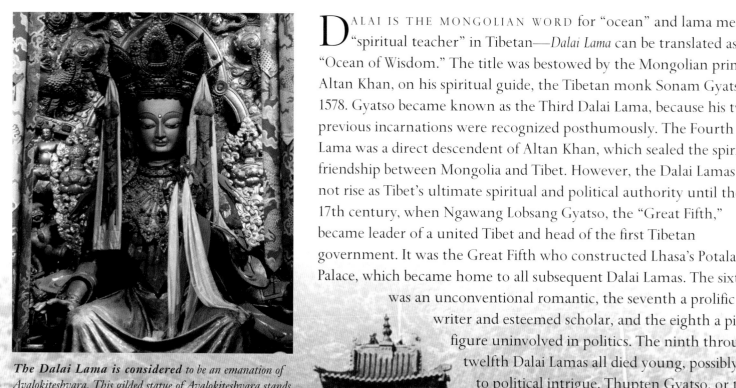

The Dalai Lama is considered to be an emanation of
Avalokiteshvara. This gilded statue of Avalokiteshvara stands
in the Jokhang, Lhasa's oldest temple, built by King Songtsen
Gampo between c. AD 637–47.

DALAI IS THE MONGOLIAN WORD for "ocean" and lama means
"spiritual teacher" in Tibetan—*Dalai Lama* can be translated as
"Ocean of Wisdom." The title was bestowed by the Mongolian prince,
Altan Khan, on his spiritual guide, the Tibetan monk Sonam Gyatso, in
1578. Gyatso became known as the Third Dalai Lama, because his two
previous incarnations were recognized posthumously. The Fourth Dalai
Lama was a direct descendent of Altan Khan, which sealed the spiritual
friendship between Mongolia and Tibet. However, the Dalai Lamas did
not rise as Tibet's ultimate spiritual and political authority until the
17th century, when Ngawang Lobsang Gyatso, the "Great Fifth,"
became leader of a united Tibet and head of the first Tibetan
government. It was the Great Fifth who constructed Lhasa's Potala
Palace, which became home to all subsequent Dalai Lamas. The sixth
was an unconventional romantic, the seventh a prolific
writer and esteemed scholar, and the eighth a pious
figure uninvolved in politics. The ninth through
twelfth Dalai Lamas all died young, possibly due
to political intrigue. Thupten Gyatso, or the

A throng of worshippers awaits
the appearance of Thupten Gyatso,
His Holiness the 13th Dalai Lama,
at a temple housing an honored
throne, Tibet, c. 1901–33.

"Great Thirteenth," as he is known, was an astute statesman and yogi, who carried Tibet into the modern world. When the Great Thirteenth died in 1933, the search began for his successor.

DISCOVERING THE DALAI LAMA

It is possible for any family, regardless of social status, to become the home for a realized being, and Dalai Lamas have been born into both noble and peasant families. The traditional way of discovering the Dalai Lama involves many complex factors. Dalai Lamas and Panchen Lamas (the second highest-ranking Tibetan spiritual figure) have recognized each other's successors since the 17th century, when Panchen Lobsang Choegyal first recognized the Fifth Dalai Lama. High lamas consult the Nechung oracle, and visit sacred sites where they receive visions. Once found, a candidate is extensively tested and is expected to identify ritual objects belonging to his former incarnation.

The Great Thirteenth, c. 1910; was a revered statesman dedicated to modernizing Tibet. In a prophetic statement made shortly before his death in 1932, he warned of the Chinese threat and predicted that the Tibetan people "will become like slaves to our conquerors, and will be made to wander helplessly like beggars."

A fresco painting depicting the 13th Dalai Lama, known as the Great Thirteenth, inside the Potala Palace in Lhasa, the traditional residence of the Dalai Lama, c. 1900.

LINEAGE OF THE DALAI LAMAS

1. Gedun Truppa (1391–1475)	8. Jampel Gyatso (1758–1804)
2. Gedun Gyatso (1475–1542)	9. Luntok Gyatso (1806–15)
3. Sonam Gyatso (1543–88)	10. Tsultrim Gyatso (1816–37)
4. Yonten Gyatso (1589–1617)	11. Khendrup Gyatso (1838–56)
5. Ngawang Lobsang Gyatso (1617–82)	12. Trinley Gyatso (1856–75)
6. Tsangyang Gyatso (1683–1706)	13. Thupten Gyatso (1876–1933)
7. Kesang Gyatso (1708–55)	14. Tenzin Gyatso (1935–)

HIS HOLINESS THE 14TH DALAI LAMA

BIOGRAPHY

T HE 14TH DALAI LAMA has traveled an extraordinary journey to become one of the most recognizable and respected figures in the world today. After the 13th Dalai Lama died in 1933, a search began for his reincarnation. The Regent of Tibet sought divine guidance in 1935 at the holy Tibetan lake of Lhamo Lhatso, where he received visions that included images of a gold-roofed monastery and a small house with odd gutters. Two years later, a search party of lamas went to the village of Takster, in Amdo province; they located the monastery, and the house, where a remarkable two-year-old boy, named Lhamo Dhondrub, lived. The head lama, a monk from Sera Monastery, disguised himself as a servant, but the boy immediately

This picture of the 14th Dalai Lama was taken in 1949 by the pioneering broadcaster Lowell Thomas, Sr., who was only the seventh American to visit Tibet at the time. He was invited by the Tibetan government to broadcast news to the West of the impending Chinese invasion, and his photographs are rare and invaluable documentation of Tibetan life before the invasion.

The Twelfth Medium of Nechung, known as the Nechung Oracle, is served by two monk attendants while he is in trance during a Monlam (New Year) ceremony at Drepung Monastery in southern India, 1983.

recognized him and identified items that had belonged to the 13th Dalai Lama, claiming that they were his. The monks were assured that the boy was the reincarnation of the Great Thirteenth, the 74th manifestation of Avalokiteshvara.

A LEADER IN TURMOIL

At the age of four, Lhamo Dhondrub was renamed Jetsun Jamphael Ngawang Lobsang Yeshe Tenzin Gyatso ("Holy Lord, Gentle Glory, Compassionate, Defender of the Faith, and Ocean of Wisdom"), and ordained as a novice monk. He moved to the Potala Palace and entered a life of strict religious study. When the Chinese invaded Tibet in 1950, the Tibetan government sought guidance from the Nechung Oracle. (For Tibetans, an oracle is a spirit who enters a human being and then acts as a medium between the physical and spiritual worlds. The Nechung or State Oracle channels the spirit of Dorje Drakden, who was bound by Padmasambhava to protect Tibet and the Dharma.) The Nechung Oracle pronounced that Tenzin Gyatso's time had come, and at 15, he was enthroned as the temporal and spiritual leader of Tibet. Four years later, he received full ordination as a Buddhist monk, and in the spring of 1959, he earned the Lharam Geshe monastic degree. After the March 10, 1959 uprising by the Tibetans was crushed by the Chinese army; with no hope of cooperation from the Chinese government, the Dalai Lama reluctantly left Tibet, escaping to India to appeal for international help. He set up a government in exile in the northern Indian town of Dharamsala. In the early 1960s, the Dalai Lama's appeal to the U.N. resulted in General Assembly resolutions that chastised China for violating Tibetan human rights. He established a Tibetan democratic constitution in 1963 and began a lifelong focus on the preservation of the Tibetan Buddhist way of life. The Dalai Lama's devotion to nonviolent methods to achieve political autonomy earned him the 1989 Nobel Peace Prize. He is a master of all four schools of Tibetan Buddhism and has widely written on the subject, although the universality of his message has made him revered as a world ambassador for peace and unity.

The 14th Dalai Lama (right) in Lhasa, 1952, with Lobsang Trinley Lhundrup Choekyi Gyaltsen—the 10th Panchen Lama and an important figure in the Tibetan struggle for freedom. Dalai Lamas and Panchen Lamas have recognized each other's incarnations since the 17th century.

The Dalai Lama escaped from Lhasa in 1959 disguised as a common Tibetan soldier, after a consultation with the Nechung Oracle indicated that he should leave. The Dalai Lama (third figure from right, in dark clothing) is shown with a small escort that included his immediate family, during the flight to India.

AN INTERVIEW WITH
HIS HOLINESS THE DALAI LAMA

Don Farber: The feeling I have is that the Buddhist way of life, whether it's Japanese, Tibetan or Thai, is something precious to help keep alive. But it seems that young Tibetans in exile, for the most part, are not so interested in Buddhism. I'm concerned about young Tibetans and their children and the future of the Tibetan Buddhist way of life.

His Holiness: Since the early sixties, Buddhism was a part of the curriculum in the Tibetan schools, starting from class one, because we felt that Tibetan society, as a whole, should have an understanding about Buddhism, real Buddhism. . . . Within Tibetan society, knowledge about Buddhism remains limited, as it has in the past. In a typical family, the practice of Buddhism is just reciting a few mantras and then offering something, but they do not know what Buddha is. In the past, for the brightest boy or girl in the family, there was no other option except to send them to a monastery or nunnery, if parents wanted them to be educated. Now, that situation is completely changed. Unless there is some enthusiasm, some interest to study Buddhism, there is no reason to join a monastery.

The important thing is the promotion of Buddhist knowledge in Tibetan society. Recently, I have been telling people that parents should be the guru of their own children. The guru in the ordinary sense—that comes much later.

If students learn the Four Noble Truths, while they learn other subjects including science, they won't find any contradictions. Many Tibetans just learn by heart a few mantras and short prayers. At worst, they believe in some kind of superstition including the controversial Shukten deity in which followers believe that all their future depends on the deity. They believe that if they make an offering of some milk or beer on their altar, this protector will help them. They have that kind of Buddhist attitude. . . . But, in the eyes of the followers of

Each morning, His Holiness does his spiritual practice here, in the shrine room of his residence at Dharamsala, 1997.

this deity, they consider this as faith, as a part of Buddhist culture. Then, the children from such families, when they study and know more about the world and science, then, of course, they lose respect for Buddhism, thinking that it is superstition. If they don't have the proper understanding of Buddhism from their family life, then later, from necessity, they become attracted to other things. They lose respect or faith in their own religion. I'm not criticizing other religions as I'm always telling people. All of them have great potential and millions of people in the past, present, future also get benefit. But other religious concepts are difficult to explain through science. So in the eyes of children, Buddhism could also be seen as a similar kind of religion. . . . Our parents, due to blind faith, consider Buddhism to be very important. But if Tibetan youth thinks that Buddhism is about blind faith or superstition, then they may think that it has no relevance in today's world.

His Holiness the Dalai Lama greets a crowd of Tibetans gathered outside of his residence in Dharamsala, in 1997; an annual appearance held every year on the morning of Losar, the Tibetan New Year.

Don Farber: I met a young woman from Kham, in Eastern Tibet, where there is tremendous faith and Buddhism is strong, but they don't have the high lamas there. So, her dream was to come to India where the high lamas are. But when she came to India she was deeply disappointed because she saw many young Tibetans uninterested in Buddhism. Gradually she began to understand that it was because of the influences of Western culture and Indian culture.

His Holiness: Now there are two kinds of Buddhist faith. In the scriptures this is also mentioned—one faith completely relies on someone, for example, saying Buddhism is good—just relying on that. This, the scriptures say, is not at all reliable, not genuine faith. The other faith, in the beginning, is the kind where one remains skeptical. Then, through study experimentation, through their own investigation, they gain some understanding. Faith that comes from your own personal conviction, is genuine faith, and we should have that kind. Now, times have changed. In the past Tibet was isolated. There was only Buddhism, except for some Bönism, and there was Islam,

His Holiness reading Buddhist scripture in his shrine room, Dharamsala, 1997.

but this was very limited . . . The majority of the population was Buddhist and took it for granted that Buddhism is best. So, there was no need for argument. But today, although we are still Tibetans, we live in an entirely different environment. Not only are there ancient, non-Buddhist philosophies, but also radical, materialist, and atheist ones. . . .

And science, to my mind, is not necessarily atheism. Science, I think, is something like seeking truth. So, it is just neutral. In comparing religions, in Christianity, they do not believe in the next life. Unlike for Buddhists, concern about the next life is no bother, not relevant. . . . In facing so many different ideas and religious influences, Buddhist study should include learning in the original Indian way. . . .One should know how Buddhism compares, have a deep knowledge of Buddhist explanations, and know what is the fault of a particular philosophy's concerns. Without that, you can't survive. So, I feel that we have the potential. We have the knowledge and the possibility

His Holiness the Dalai Lama *stands on a balcony at the Vietnamese Buddhist Temple, Los Angeles, 1989, left, throwing rice to a joyous crowd below; each grain of rice carries his blessings.*

Geshe Gyelsten, *director of the Thubten Dharge Ling Buddhist Center, presented His Holiness with a ritual offering, right, at the conclusion of an empowerment given by His Holiness in Los Angeles, 2000.*

of being able to do that, to survive within other existing beliefs or ideologies, but, we are actually following a more or less conservative path and just doing things that were done in the past in Tibet, not taking into consideration the changed circumstances and situations.

For quite a number of years, I suggested that the big monasteries . . . should study living, non-Buddhist philosophies and religions, including Islam, Christianity, Judaism, and Hinduism, as well as Western philosophy from Greek philosophy up to Bertrand Russell. But so far this has not been implemented. You can't blame them. There have not been Tibetan teachers who have studied these philosophies. Now, in the future, some Tibetans who know English and have studied Western philosophy and religion, they could explain through our own language, about Western thought on modern non-Buddhist schools and philosophies. This should be done. So, these are some of the long-term ways I've thought of to preserve the Tibetan Buddhist tradition.

Don Farber: Can I be so bold as to make a suggestion?

His Holiness: Yes, of course.

Don Farber: In my work researching Buddhist cultures, I've spent time with young Buddhist associations in Taiwan, Thailand, and Indonesia, where they gather at their own coffee houses to discuss Dharma activities and things they can do in the community. Groups like these could develop branches in other Tibetan settlements in India and Nepal, as well as in the United States, with a focus on keeping Tibetan Buddhism alive and growing in their minds.

His Holiness: Oh yes, excellent. Just a few weeks ago, in order to promote Buddhist understanding in our various settlements, I suggested . . . rather than having a lama there as a teacher, invite any family member who has an interest in Buddhism. Come together and then talk, a casual sort of talk: what are the Four Noble Truths, what are the differences between Buddha and Jesus Christ . . . what are the differences, and with Mohammed, like that. Just a sort of social gathering and discussion. . . . I think someone should take the initiative. Once some kind of nucleus is formed, among the officials or staff members here or in the schools and settlements, we can provide some materials and, if necessary, financial help. So occasionally, say every third Sunday or Saturday evening, we could have tea and talk about Buddhist culture, about Buddhist spirituality. Just as you suggested about Buddhist youth groups in other countries, it's very important that something like this should also happen amongst the Tibetan community so that people, out of their own interest, are able to discuss and learn more about Buddhism.

At the closing ceremony of a tantric retreat in Dharamsala, 1997, His Holiness performs a fire puja, a ceremony where ritual substances are thrown into flames. Fire pujas perform different functions; at the end of retreats, they are meant to purify any errors made by practitioners and to strengthen their connection with the retreat deity.

Don Farber: In L.A., there are many rinpoches who give teachings, but Tibetans don't go because they feel uncomfortable about being addressed in English. Maybe when the rinpoches come they could spend time with just the Tibetans and speak Tibetan with them. Yet in the settlements, you have wonderful lamas, but the young people rarely hear any Dharma from them. Why is that?

His Holiness: It's true. Tibetan youth in the '60s and early '70s openly criticized Tibetan Buddhism. Now today, I don't think anyone will. The Tibetan generation of those early days, as well as the Chinese, must find it very intriguing that in the West, at least in the academic world, professors and people in the most respected educational institutions are showing interest in taking teachings from some stupid, dirty Tibetan lama! (laughter) . . . Of course, you can't say all these scholars and scientists are stupid or crazy. So I entirely agree. We really need more effort. Some of the lamas who are teaching in the West, are not considered lamas among Tibetan society and may not be highly respected. They don't have that kind of recognition. (His Holiness says this with much laughter). Good! Goodbye.

MASTERS OF TIBETAN BUDDHISM

བོད་ཀྱི་ནང་པའི་སྒྲུབ་དབོན་རྣམས་ཀྱི་སྐོར།

EVEN SHAKYAMUNI BUDDHA needed the guidance of teachers on his journey to enlightenment. In a popular analogy, the spiritual practitioner is likened to a patient. The Buddhist teachings or "Dharma" is the medicine. The sicknesses are mental and emotional afflictions, and the guru is the physician. The living presence of the spiritual master makes the ideal of Buddhahood an accessible and tangible reality, and provides an inspirational role model to which the disciple can aspire. Practitioners may receive instruction from numerous teachers, but there is generally a "root guru" with whom they develop a special relationship. Unlike other Buddhist traditions, in Tibetan Buddhism, after enlightened masters die, they can be rediscovered as incarnate masters. Such extraordinary gurus, called *rinpoches* or "precious jewels," are at the very heart of Tibetan Buddhist life.

His Holiness Penor Rinpoche, throne holder of the Palyul lineage of the Nyingma tradition, gives blessings to a Tibetan woman during the Nyingma Monlam at Bodhgaya, India, in 1997.

His Holiness Mindroling Rinpoche is the head of the Nyingma tradition of Tibetan Buddhism. This portrait was taken in Clementown, India, in 1997.

INCARNATE MASTERS

UNIQUE TO TIBETAN BUDDHISM is the system of recognizing reincarnated masters, the Dalai Lama being the most famous example. The term *Rinpoche* (pronounced rimpochey), is a reverential title given to incarnate masters who are also referred to as *tulkus.* They are living repositories of Vajrayana Buddhist traditions, voluntarily being reborn lifetime after lifetime in the same role to continue to transmit the Dharma to others. Buddhists believe that all of us have had untold former lives, not just as humans but as animals and beings who exist in other realms. Although all practitioners work to develop the karmic causes for a favorable rebirth as a human (the most conducive form for spiritual development), most have no direct control over the specific conditions of their future lives. Highly realized practitioners, however, are able to choose the time, place and circumstance of their death as well as the conditions of their next life.

During the Kalachakra initiation given by His Holiness the Dalai Lama near Siliguri, India, in 1997, a number of incarnate masters participated in the ceremony.

THE TULKU SYSTEM

Formerly in Tibet, there were around 3,000 tulkus (though many did not survive the Chinese invasion), and today, lineage heads and knowledge holders continue to take rebirth to share their wisdom with the world. Tulkus are generally discovered when they are children and undergo a process of recognition, enthronement, and training before they are formally invested with the spiritual responsibilities of their lineage. The authenticity of a tulku is determined according to a strict procedure, which includes the meditational experiences of high lamas, consultation with oracles and other forms of divination, and the direct testing of the candidate. In the test, a potential tulku is asked to pick out articles that belonged to their previous incarnation from among other similar objects. At an early age these tulkus demonstrate a remarkable ability to absorb and learn whatever they are taught, as if they had mastered these subjects before and were just being refreshed. They often appear to recognize their students from their previous life.

The process of recognizing tulkus ensures that student-mentor relationships can remain throughout many lifetimes, creating an unbroken continuum of instruction and learning that transcends time and space. Although students grieve when their masters pass away, they know that this is not the end, and work to create the karmic causes to meet their teacher again—if not during this life, then in the next. This process also, to some degree, diminished the influence of the aristocracy in Tibet, as tulkus were discovered in families from every social class. Along with tulkus, the Tibetan Buddhist tradition has produced many extraordinary scholars and meditation masters or *yogis*. Some of these masters, *khenpos* for example (see next page), are also called *rinpoche* or "precious jewel," although they may not have been recognized as tulkus.

His Holiness the late 16th Karmapa at the Vietnamese Buddhist Temple in Los Angeles, in 1977.

On His Holiness the 17th Karmapa's birthday in 1997, monks in northern India show reverence for their guru, who was still in Tibet. In 2000, the young 17th Karmapa escaped to India.

OTHER TYPES OF MASTERS

IN THE NYINGMA, KAGYU, AND SAKYA traditions, the title of *khenpo* is used to indicate someone who has attained an extraordinary level of Buddhist scholastic training, equivalent to a doctorate degree in Buddhist philosophy. The training encompasses a complete theoretical education in Buddhism and requires a 9- to 15-year study program. In the Gelug school, khenpo is the title of the senior master who presides over the ordination ceremony of new monks, and is often used to denote an abbot of a monastic college. The abbot is appointed either by a high lama such as the Dalai Lama or by senior members of the monastic community, and must also be a *geshe*. Geshe means "spiritual friend," and is the highest degree in the Gelug system. Like khenpos, geshes are held in high esteem for their superior scholarship. However, very few monks who begin the training program actually earn the degree, as it takes from 15 to 25 years of intensive study to complete. To earn the highest degree of Lharam Geshe, the student must go through an oral examination in front of the Dalai Lama and other eminent Gelug masters. The "finals" occur during the Monlam festival, when candidates must again demonstrate their understanding of Buddhist scripture through philosophical debate. Upon completion of their studies, geshes may enter into a three-year retreat.

The late Nyoshul Khen Rinpoche, *who was a revered khenpo in the Nyingma lineage, attended the Nyingma Monlam at Bodhgaya in 1997.*

RETREAT

From the Buddhist point of view, retreat is not an escape from the world, but a formidable venture free of distractions and worldly comforts that can hinder spiritual development. Many Tibetan Buddhist practitioners eventually enter into solitary retreat to hone their spiritual understanding. A particular yogi lineage are the *togdens* who live in isolated huts or caves and practice a unique form of yoga. These yogis live a spartan existence and engage in intensive meditation practices for many years, and sometimes their entire lives. *Ngakpas* are lay practitioners and householders who are masters of Dzogchen. Although a Ngakpa may marry and have children he must spend a great deal of time in retreat.

Venerable Geshe Tsephel, *left, in Santa Cruz, California, 1989, is now a khenpo or abbot of the Gelug, Ganden Jangtse Buddhist monastery in India.*

Venerable Togden Amting, *a yogi, in his hut in Himachal Pradesh, India, 1997, right. He has lived there in retreat for many years.*

FUNERAL OF KALU RINPOCHE

ALU RINPOCHE WAS ONE OF THE GREATEST Tibetan Buddhist masters of our time. Many revered teachers studied under him, including His Holiness the 16th Karmapa. Born in Kham, Eastern Tibet, in 1905, Kalu Rinpoche was believed to be an emanation of Milarepa, the great Tibetan yogi, and like Milarepa, he spent twelve years in isolated retreat in mountainous regions of Tibet. After the Chinese invasion, he left Tibet in 1957, and spent a few years teaching in Bhutan. In following years, he established a network of Karma Kagyu monasteries and Dharma centers in India, Europe, and the United States, and a number of Tibetan and Western practitioners undertook three-year retreats under his guidance. Kalu Rinpoche came to the United States for the last time in 1988, and his students gathered from all over North America to be with him. The quality of Kalu Rinpoche's teaching was so profound that even near to his death, he was able to communicate the Dharma with absolute clarity and lucidity. But it was clear that his health was ailing, and there was an unspoken understanding that his students were seeing their guru for the last time in his present incarnation.

Kalu Rinpoche sat for this portrait in 1988, in Pasadena, near Los Angeles, a few months before his death.

A monk at Sonada Monastery beats a gong to call his fellow monks to prayer during the funeral for Kalu Rinpoche, Darjeeling, India, 1989.

Two Tibetan Buddhist masters, *Beru Khyentse Rinpoche and Gyaltsab Rinpoche, in the shrine room of Kalu Rinpoche's residence at Sonada Monastery in Darjeeling. They are performing rituals and chanting in front of the* kudung, *a decorated large wooden chest holding Kalu Rinpoche's body, preserved in salt. Chanting sessions and ceremonies were held by monks and laypeople for 49 days following his death.*

PREPARATION FOR BARDO

A few months later, it became known that Kalu Rinpoche had passed away, and disciples from his various centers around the world began to make preparations to attend the funeral at his monastery, near Darjeeling, India. After flying into Calcutta and taking the Darjeeling mail train up to Siliguri, they took jeeps and taxis into the mountains and through tea plantations, to the monastery in the little roadside village of Sonada. A large group of monks were gathered, and there was a feeling of camaraderie as they were reunited with those whom they had trained with years before. Inside the main hall, the monks, some as young as five years old, chanted and played horns and gongs for the services that went on all day and evening for 49 days—the maximum length of time that the consciousness is believed to take on its passage through the *bardo* to a new rebirth. In the *bardo,* a person becomes a mental being whose reality is created by thought alone, a confusing and frightening episode for the spiritually unprepared. After the bardo period, an ordinary person is thrown into their next rebirth by the force of their past karmic actions. A highly realized master, however, can exercise mental control and direct the circumstances of his or her next rebirth.

Sonada is a place that gets a tremendous amount of moisture, and the rain and fog created an atmosphere of serenity and introspection, as disciples focused on their responsibility to assist in the ceremonies, knowing that their prayers and recitations were helping their master to return swiftly to this world. As the regent of the Karmapa, Tai Situ Rinpoche, said during this time, "When a great master dies, we Tibetans are not so sad, because it is as if they've only gone on a vacation." Tai Situ's words seemed to give comfort and clarity to everyone present. All Buddhist practices can be viewed as a preparation for the time of death, and the only thing that will help us when we die, say Tibetan masters, is our spiritual practice. Tibetans do not celebrate birthdays, but they do honor the death-days of great masters, as it is believed that this is when they realized the highest spiritual attainment. The congregation was joined by many people from Bhutan, including members of the Bhutanese royal family, as well as people from the Tamang hill tribe, which has a large population around Darjeeling. Kalu Rinpoche had also been teacher to the regents of the Karmapa, including Tai Situ Rinpoche and Gyeltsup Rinpoche, as well as the late Jamyang Khongtrol Rinpoche. All of these eminent masters came to participate in his funeral along with Kalu Rinpoche's chief disciple, Bokar Rinpoche, the lama responsible for overseeing the monasteries and training of monks and nuns until the coming of age of his master's reincarnation. Every day when the masters entered the main hall, they were led by a procession of monks blowing Tibetan horns, and everyone paused and bowed in reverence as they passed.

Kalu Rinpoche's kudung, in state at Sonada Monastery, below, adorned with flowers, candles, khatas, and brocade. Disciples from all over the world came to the funeral.

*Two young **monks** light butter lamps during the funeral services, above.*

FINAL DAYS OF THE CEREMONY

About one week before the end of the 49-day period, the kudung holding Kalu Rinpoche's body was taken in a procession from his residence into the main hall. As the final days approached, the intensity of the chanting and rituals increased. They were now being performed continuously 24 hours a day, with shifts of people taking turns to keep the chanting constant. As the people concentrated on their spiritual practice, most remained calm and composed, but among the crowd, a Bhutanese woman named Kalzang Drolkar was crying. She and her husband, Lama Gyaltsen (who was also Kalu Rinpoche's nephew), had been Rinpoche's caretakers. The night before the final day of the funeral, the monks lit hundreds of butter lamps to "dispel the darkness of ignorance."

Above a sea of clouds, *monks lead the procession that brought Kalu Rinpoche's kudung back to his residence on the 49th day of the funeral, right.*

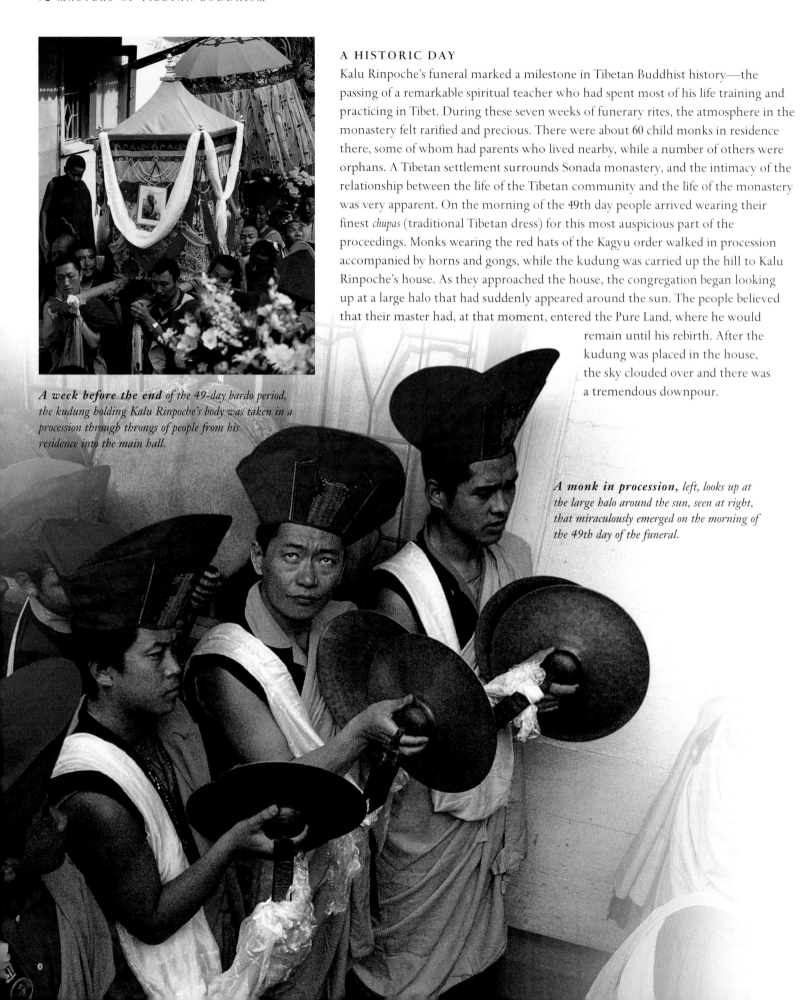

A week before the end of the 49-day bardo period, the kudung holding Kalu Rinpoche's body was taken in a procession through throngs of people from his residence into the main hall.

A HISTORIC DAY

Kalu Rinpoche's funeral marked a milestone in Tibetan Buddhist history—the passing of a remarkable spiritual teacher who had spent most of his life training and practicing in Tibet. During these seven weeks of funerary rites, the atmosphere in the monastery felt rarified and precious. There were about 60 child monks in residence there, some of whom had parents who lived nearby, while a number of others were orphans. A Tibetan settlement surrounds Sonada monastery, and the intimacy of the relationship between the life of the Tibetan community and the life of the monastery was very apparent. On the morning of the 49th day people arrived wearing their finest *chupas* (traditional Tibetan dress) for this most auspicious part of the proceedings. Monks wearing the red hats of the Kagyu order walked in procession accompanied by horns and gongs, while the kudung was carried up the hill to Kalu Rinpoche's house. As they approached the house, the congregation began looking up at a large halo that had suddenly appeared around the sun. The people believed that their master had, at that moment, entered the Pure Land, where he would remain until his rebirth. After the kudung was placed in the house, the sky clouded over and there was a tremendous downpour.

A monk in procession, left, looks up at the large halo around the sun, seen at right, that miraculously emerged on the morning of the 49th day of the funeral.

REINCARNATION OF KALU RINPOCHE

About a year after Kalu Rinpoche's death, his former attendants, Kalzang Drolkar and her husband, Lama Gyaltsen, had a son. In 1992, when the boy was two years old, it was revealed that he was the incarnation of their guru. Upon hearing the news, Lama Gyaltsen prostrated before his child and their relationship was transformed from that moment on. The boy became the student of Bokar Rinpoche—who had been his student in his previous life—and stayed with him at his monastery in Mirik, in the district of Darjeeling. In 1995, Bokar Rinpoche and the young Kalu Rinpoche came to the United States, where Bokar Rinpoche gave teachings in Santa Monica, California, and many of Kalu Rinpoche's former students came to greet his new incarnation.

The young Kalu Rinpoche

The six-year-old tulku sat on a throne alongside the elder master, and remained almost motionless for several hours while the teaching was given. This has been the only visit to the United States by the new Kalu Rinpoche, who for several years now has been receiving intensive spiritual education in India, including personal instruction from His Holiness the Dalai Lama. The Dalai Lama and the previous Kalu Rinpoche had deep respect for one another. Since the new Kalu Rinpoche's visit, his father has passed away, and his mother returned to Bhutan. Kalu Rinpoche will continue to receive very careful training over the next years before he begins to give teachings.

MONLAM FOR WORLD PEACE

THE GREAT PRAYER FESTIVAL of Monlam Chenmo was established in 1409 by Tsongkhapa, the founder of the Gelug school, and became an important annual Tibetan event. Shortly after the New Year celebrations of Losar, tens of thousands of monastics would come to the capital of Lhasa from all over the country and from as far away as Mongolia, Nepal, Bhutan, Sikkim, and Siberia to gather in the central hall of the Johkang, Tibet's most holy temple. In front of the sacred Jowo Buddha statue, the congregation would engage in prayers and practices day and night for a period of fifteen days, chanting praises to the Buddha and performing sacred dances, while dedicating the merits for others' happiness. It was during Monlam that the candidates for the Gelug school's highest degree of Geshe Lharam would take their final examinations in front of the Dalai Lama, proving the extent of their spiritual understanding in philosophical debates. All the residents of Lhasa would use this time to intensify their spiritual practice by making butter lamp offerings, performing prostrations and circumambulations, and giving alms.

The young Thong Thong Tulku Rinpoche, *above, along with many other monks, attended the Nyingma Monlam at Bodhgaya in 1997.*

The late Venerable *Khenpo Thubten Mewa Rinpoche, left, one of the Nyingma tradition's most revered masters, was greeted by a friend at the Nyingma Monlam at Bodhgaya, in 1997.*

MONLAM IN EXILE

The Monlam festival commemorates the Buddha's "Great Miracle," when he was challenged to prove his supernatural abilities in a contest of magic. The Buddha completely awed his opponents by performing miraculous feats such as manifesting infinite duplicates of his body, with fire blazing from each one. Thus, the Monlam festival is connected with the New Year tradition of driving out negative forces in the context of protecting and preserving the Dharma. Perceiving the festival to encourage Tibetan nationalism, the Chinese authorities banned Monlam celebrations after 1959. The festival resumed briefly in the 1980s, and was again prohibited in 1990. The activities that are permitted in Tibet today bear little relevance to the festival's original spirit. The first Monlam in exile was held in 1961 at Bodhghaya, when 500 refugee monks gathered to pray for the harmony of the world and the welfare of all

The late Venerable Azing Rinpoche attended the Nyingma Monlam at Bodhgaya in 1997.

sentient beings. In exile, each of the four schools of Tibetan Buddhism has their own Monlam, which they celebrate within a few weeks of one another each winter. The Gelug Monlam is held in Dharamsala while the Sakya Monlam takes place at Lumbini in Nepal, the Buddha's birthplace. The Nyingma and Kagyu Monlams are held in Bodhgaya. At the Nyingma Monlam, the lineage masters sit facing each of the four sides of the Mahabodhi Stupa, with the monks and nuns of each lineage behind them. Every day for two weeks, several thousand monks, nuns, and lay people perform *pujas* (ritual offerings). A seemingly continuous stream of mostly Tibetans circumambulate the great stupa, which at dusk is illuminated by thousands of butter lamps. Prayers are made for the longevity of the Three Jewels—the Buddha, Dharma, and Sangha—and to promote understanding, harmony, and peace among all peoples.

HIS HOLINESS SAKYA TRIZIN

HIS HOLINESS SAKYA TRIZIN is the 41st in an unbroken lineage of lamas going back to AD 1073. He was born in Tibet in 1945 and received his first major empowerment at the age of three. Two years later, he traveled to Ngor Ewam Choden Monastery and received teachings from the abbot, who became his root guru. The young boy possessed an extraordinary ability to recite Buddhist texts by heart, and when he was eight years old he entered a seven-month retreat. In 1959, at the age of fourteen, he was formally enthroned as the Sakya Trizin, head of the Sakya school. He fled Tibet the same year, and was given support by the Royal Court of Sikkim. Since then he has taught all over the world and has founded numerous monasteries and institutes for Buddhist higher studies, including Sakya College in Rajpur, India, where he resides. His Holiness Sakya Trizin works tirelessly to preserve the Tibetan Buddhist teachings. He is known for his eloquence and his ability to communicate the Dharma to people from all backgrounds and walks of life.

Q: Your Holiness, what are the problems in trying to preserve the Tibetan Buddhist way of life?

A: The main problem is that Tibetans have lost their country and are now living in exile, scattered throughout the world. . . . Due to this, we face many difficulties in preserving our way of life, tradition, and cultural heritage.

Q: What is being done to preserve this rich cultural and religious heritage?

A: Under the leadership of His Holiness the Dalai Lama and many other religious leaders, we have already started many monasteries in India and Nepal as well as many Dharma centers throughout the world. There are also many institutions were one can learn Buddhism and schools where one can learn Tibetan reading, writing, and basic education as well as higher philosophies. The most important thing is for Tibetans to be able to freely reside in Tibet so that all the Tibetans are living together. Through being together we can do many things to promote the Buddhist teachings as well as the Tibetan cultural heritage.

Q: Why is Buddhist practice and study important?

A: Buddhist practice and study is important, especially in this modern age, because it is a very logical philosophy. Buddha himself said that his teachings should be examined just as we would examine gold. When we go to buy gold, we make sure that it is genuine, and only when we are convinced that it is genuine, do we buy it.

Q: Can Your Holiness please give one important message regarding Dharma?

A: Basically the Dharma means not harming any sentient beings. The Lord Buddha gave many teachings, but at the moment there are two main traditions, the Hinayana and the Mahayana. In the Hinayana tradition, the main idea is not to harm any sentient beings, from the tiniest of insects up to human beings or Devas (celestial beings or gods). In the Mahayana tradition, one should not only avoid harming beings but one should also be of benefit to other sentient beings. In this way, by abstaining from harming sentient beings and also by benefiting and helping sentient beings through kindness and compassion, one can experience real peace, harmony and happiness . . . . to be able to do this is therefore the development of compassion. To practice

compassion is most important for the sake of future lives as well as this life, for oneself and for all other beings.

Q: How important is the relationship between a Rinpoche and his disciple?

A: The *guru-chela* (master-disciple) relationship is very important. Without the teacher, one cannot find the spiritual path. And even once one has entered the path, it is very important to have the guru's guidance. In every Buddhist tradition, the relationship between the guru and disciple is very important.

Q: Are there any important or special experiences with your masters that revealed some fundamental truth that had a profound effect on your life?

A: All the masters are very important, but they cannot reveal the fundamental truths as if they are just showing an object. Instead, they give many teachings on how one can realize the ultimate truth. It is not easy, of course; it is something very difficult and a very long process. I am still very far from realization. In order to realize the ultimate truth, we must accumulate merit as well as wisdom. According to [the teachings of] my own spiritual masters, I am trying my best to accumulate the merit and wisdom through which I will be able to eventually realize the ultimate truth.

Q: One last question. What is the difference between empowerment and teaching?

A: Empowerment is only in the Vajrayana teachings. After receiving the common teachings, then those who are capable enter into what we call Vajrayana or Tantric Buddhism. In order to practice Tantric Buddhism, one has to receive initiations or empowerments. If one tries to practice the Vajrayana or Tantric teachings without receiving the empowerments, then it is of more harm than benefit. These empowerments are a very special ceremony during which you are enrolled into the Vajrayana path. After initiation one can then receive the more advanced teachings.

Los Angeles, 1989

HIS HOLINESS THE 100TH GANDEN TRI RINPOCHE

LOBSANG NYIMA held the title of the 100th Ganden Tri Rinpoche (Holder of the Ganden Throne and the official head of the Gelug School of Tibetan Buddhism), a seven-year office, until 2003. Born in 1921 in Kham, eastern Tibet, he became a monk at Ganden Jangtse monastery near Lhasa at the age of twelve, transferring five years later to Drepung Loseling Monastery near Lhasa for further teaching. He followed the Dalai Lama into exile to India in 1959 and continued his training, eventually earning the Lharam Geshe, the highest degree in the Gelug tradition. He was later appointed abbot of Gyumey Tantric College and then of Namgyal Dratsang, the Dalai Lama's private monastery. In 1995, he assumed the title Ganden Tri Rinpoche, where he oversaw the training of Gelug monks worldwide, from Depung Loseling Monastery in Mundgod, India.

Q: Can you speak about the preservation of the Tibetan Buddhist way of life?
A: The Tibetan culture and way of life is passing through one of its most crucial times. The old Tibetan traditions are gradually facing a slow erosion. If people find that this age-old Tibetan tradition is of some use to the world as a whole then it does not matter whether the people who are striving for its upkeep are Tibetans or not. If there is a person who truly feels that this tradition, if lost, will be a great loss to the whole of mankind, then, they should help it or else there is no other reason for clinging on to it like some kind of wealth or land. So, with Tibetans in front and working with others who agree with this idea, together, they should work hard to preserve this culture. And, if you feel this way about our culture then I am very happy to know it. And, if you are doing this not for personal gains but for the well-being of all, then, it is very good.

Drepung Losseling Monastery,
Mundgod, southern India, 1997

"If there is a person who truly feels that this tradition if lost will be a great loss to the whole of mankind, then, they should help it or else there is no other reason for clinging on to it like some kind of wealth or land."

KHENPO KUNGA WANGCHUK RINPOCHE

RENOWNED AS ONE OF THE Sakya tradition's greatest masters, Khenpo Kunga Wangchuk Rinpoche studied under the great Jamyang Khyentse Chokyi Lodro at Dzongsar Monastery in Tibet. Following the Chinese invasion, and the destruction of Dzongsar Monastery, he spent 23 years in prison. He came to India in 1983 to head the Dzongsar Institute in Himachal Pradesh, India. The institute was built by Dzongsar Khyentse Rinpoche, who is recognized as an incarnation of Jamyang Khyentse. Under Khenpo Kunga Wangchuk's guidance, the Institute has continued the nonsectarian approach to Tibetan Buddhism known as Rime, which was taught by Jamyang Khyentse. His Holiness the Dalai Lama has received teachings from Khenpo Kunga Wangchuk, who now stays mainly in retreat.

Q: How can Tibetan Buddhist traditions be continued for future generations?
A: I consider it very important that elder Tibetans, whether they are lay people or of the monastic order, who have knowledge about Tibetan Buddhism, they should try as far as possible to give guidance to the younger generation about their rich cultural heritage and religion. Only then will the Buddhist values and way of life not erode and only then will we be able to revive all that has been lost and make Buddhism flourish once again. So, it is the elder peoples' responsibility to constantly give guidance.

Dzongsar Monastery, Himachal Pradesh, India, 1997

> "The main merit of the practice of Buddhism is in the improvement or the evolution of the mind and the way of thinking."

If a young Tibetan is not that much interested in Buddhism, then, others should guide him towards religion by telling him the importance of Buddhism. He should be told the merits of its practice and the hardships one will suffer if one does not practice it. This is what I believe.

Q: Why is the study and practice of Buddhism important?
A: The main merit of the practice of Buddhism is in the improvement or the evolution of the mind and the way of thinking. It stops evil thoughts and instills the power of positive thinking. This will bring, in this life, a harmonious coexistence with all sentient beings. It will end the will to harm, it brings peace, and instills the will to help and to be compassionate and caring. This thought will grow during a man's life, during his death, after his death, even when he is reborn, and through many other rebirths until finally reaching the ultimate aim of Buddhist practice which is enlightenment which will be devoid of any suffering be it of the body or of the spirit. These are the merits of Buddhism which are not only for this life but also for all the coming lives until the attainment of Buddhahood.

> "It stops evil thoughts and instills the power of positive thinking."

HIS EMINENCE GARCHIN RINPOCHE

HIS EMINENCE GARCHEN RINPOCHE was born in Eastern Tibet and was recognized as an incarnate master when he was very young. He was brought to the Lho Miyal Monastery at age 7. Studying and practicing under great masters, Garchen Rinpoche received a broad range of teachings in the Drikung Kagyu lineage. At age 22, shortly before completing the traditional three-year retreat, Garchen Rinpoche was imprisoned in a labor camp by the Chinese where he spent the next 20 years. While in prison, he secretly received teachings from his fellow inmate, the great Nyingma master Khenpo Munsel. Since his release in 1979, Garchen Rinpoche has made great efforts to rebuild the Drikung Kagyu monasteries and reestablish the Buddhist teachings in Eastern Tibet. Now residing at his Dharma center in Chino Valley, Arizona, Rinpoche is renowned for his vast realization as well as his great kindness.

Q: What is the essence of Tibetan Buddhism and your work?

A: The Buddhist idea is to be helpful and kind and refrain from harming all sentient beings. There are many teachings of Buddha but here is only one essence: the two altruistic minds of enlightenment—conventional and ultimate *bodhicitta*. In order to achieve ultimate bodhicitta one needs to actualize conventional bodhicitta by seeing all sentient beings as one's own parents and not feeling jealousy, anger or any negative emotions towards them. Thinking about the benefit of others is the primary concern and the primary practice of Buddhists and the way of peace. Ignorance is the root cause of all suffering because ignorance brings delusion which causes suffering.

Teaching the law of causality and its fruition (karma) to others is my primary practice. By understanding the laws of cause and effect one will come to recognize that all the experiences of pleasure and pain are the result of one's own past actions. If one experiences pain and suffering, that experience is the result of past misdeeds. If one experiences pleasure and joy, that experience is the result of past good deeds. The root of all the good deeds is the practice of boddhicitta.

Even though other religious traditions teach love and compassion, there are differences in the scope of its practice. Buddhism teaches how to develop love and compassion toward all sentient beings while other religious traditions' teachings of love and compassion are limited only to human beings. I teach others to refrain from causing suffering to other fellow sentient beings. Whenever and wherever I go, this is what I teach and tell others.

Q: Could you speak about the importance of preserving the Tibetan Buddhist way of life.

A: Tibetan Buddhism is very, very deep. Millions of buddhas have come in the past. In this eon seven buddhas will come; Shakyamuni Buddha is the recent one. For all these buddhas of the past, present, and future there is no difference or change in the qualities of their bodhicitta. The essence of Buddhism is bodhicitta. What is bodhicitta? It is to eliminate all the self-centered thoughts and attachment to self and to generate and develop a strong desire to benefit and help others.

Q: What one thing would you like to tell western students?

A: Westerners are highly educated and have high levels of material comfort but seem to have difficulties acquiring mental peace. To attain freedom from mental and emotional suffering,

one needs to understand the Law of Causality and its Results which affect everyone regardless of whether one is rich or poor. If one has understanding of the Law of Causality and Its Results, that person will be very calm and peaceful. For people to love to hear about how to develop love and compassion and Laws of Causality, that is the main thing.

Q: How were you able to continue your practice of compassion and control your anger in prison?

A: Bodhicitta is the cause of attaining Buddhahood. One makes commitment to never let go of bodhicitta for many life times. Anger, pride, and jealousy are the cause of losing bodhicitta. If one loses bodhicitta, one would lose their way to Buddhahood. One is going against the teaching of Buddha. Buddha said, all experiences are due to one's own past action and the result of past misdeeds. If one has bodhicitta, for instance in prison, one can help others who are suffering by practicing generosity in giving them such things as food and clothing. In this way one would have the mind of practicing generosity and of not harming others. When faced with difficulties, one can practice patience. One can have thoughts of helping others every day in prison, for instance, while making bricks which will help others to build homes or while working in the field farming which will provide food for others. Thinking that way may have helped increase the practice of bodhicitta and not have caused it to degenerate.

The main thing was that one was not allowed to read Buddhist texts or recite prayers. But mind is the principle factor. Without reading texts and reciting prayers, one can focus on the meditations of bodhicitta and the four immeasurable thoughts by contemplating that all sentient beings have been one's own parents. There isn't a single person in this world that has not been one's parents. Getting angry with others will only hurt oneself. During the day you worked and at night you meditated on love, compassion, and bodhicitta. That was the life.

Monterey Park, California, 1988

GESHE TSULTIM GYELTSEN

BORN IN EASTERN TIBET in 1923, Geshe Gyeltsen studied from age seven to age sixteen under Geshe Jampa Thaye, from Sera Monastery in Tibet. He later studied at Ganden Monastery until the Chinese invasion, when he escaped into India. Eventually he earned the highest Gelug degree of Lharam Geshe. In 1963 he traveled to Sussex, England, with 22 Tibetan children, mostly orphans or children of prisoners being held by the Chinese. He instructed them for seven years in the Tibetan language, culture, and Buddhism. In 1975 he moved to the United States, and established Thubten Dhargye Ling Monastery in Long Beach, California. He has also established centers in Texas, Colorado, and Mexico. He actively works for Tibetan human rights and helps to support a Tibetan home for the home in South India.

Q: Could you share what you believe to be the most important message of the Dharma?
A: In Tibetan Buddhism, we recognize that not only us human beings, but all other beings in the world, share the same innate wish for happiness and goodness. We all share this wish. The thing is that happiness does not arise without causes and conditions. In order to have happiness we need to create its cause, which usually means engaging in positive actions. We need to do that.

In Tibetan Buddhism, we consider that at a very personal level, and also at the collective level, we need to follow the law of karma properly. This means that if we are seeking positive results, we should create positive actions. If we don't want negative results, we should not perform negative actions. In this regard, the historical teacher, Shakyamuni Buddha has very clearly and unambiguously stated in a sutra, "Do not commit any negativity, accumulate the wealth of virtue or positive actions, subdue your mind. This is the teaching of the Buddha."

Venerable Geshe Gyeltsen giving a mandala offering, Los Angeles, 1995. Concentric gold or silver rings are stacked with grains, stones, and precious jewels, representing all the objects of desire. This is visualized as a pure universe that is offered to the buddhas without any attachment, to benefit all sentient beings.

Based on our own personal wishes and experience of "I want happiness and do not want any kind of suffering," we have to recognize that everyone else has these same wishes. To whatever extent we can help them and benefit them we should do that. Even if we can not benefit them, we should see that we do not harm them.

> "In order to have happiness we need to create its cause, which usually means engaging in positive actions. We need to do that."

See, in Tibetan Buddhism, we talk about the ideal of the bodhisattva's way of life, which is basically focusing on cherishing other beings and giving less importance to oneself. We try to counteract our self-cherishing attitude. If we can cherish all others much more than ourselves, then that's the best thing. But even if we can't do that, at least we can orient out attitude towards

the hope that eventually we will be able to cherish them. As it is stated in the Eight Verses of Mind Training, "May I see all beings as a wish-fulfilling gem. Seeing the importance of everyone, may I both day in and day out be able to cherish others." In the Lojong or Mind Training texts, it says that we should take the suffering of others and the cause of their suffering upon ourselves, and we should give to others our happiness and the cause of happiness. This is what we call the *tonglen* practice—the practice of giving and taking. Shakyamuni Buddha practiced in this way, and he eventually became a Buddha—a fully enlightened being. So, we as followers should also take that first step and hope that one day, like Buddha, we will also be able to cherish others.

LAMA THARCHIN RINPOCHE

VENERABLE LAMA THARCHIN RINPOCHE is a Dzogchen (Great Perfection) master of Vajrayana Buddhism. He is the tenth lineage holder of the Repkong Ngakpas. This is a family lineage of yogis that was the largest community of nonmonastic practitioners in Tibet. Rinpoche was trained in His Holiness Dudjom Rinpoche's monastery, completing the three-year retreat and then spending another five years in solitary retreat. He left Tibet by foot with his family in 1959 and lived in India and Nepal before coming to America in 1984 for health reasons. While in America, Dudjom Rinpoche asked him to turn the third wheel of Dharma, the teachings of Vajrayana Buddhism. In addition to Dudjom Rinpoche, his main teachers have been Chatral Rinpoche, Lama Sherab Dorje Rinpoche, and Dungse Thinley Norbu Rinpoche.

Q: Could you talk about the preservation of Tibetan culture and the Buddhist way of life?
A: All of Buddha's teachings were translated into Tibetan: Hinayana, Mahayana, Vajrayana, as well as the Great Perfection due to the kindness of Guru Rinpoche [Padmasambhava]. There were so many incredible beings—*Mahasiddhas,* scholars, translators, and realized practitioners. Many yogis and monks attained rainbow body. When they died they turned to rainbow light, and then disappeared into space. In one monastery alone, it was recorded that over 100,000 monks attained rainbow body.

All of Tibetan culture is based on the Dharma. In other countries there is a part of the population that practices a religion, but Tibet was one hundred percent Buddhist. These days, Tibetan culture and Dharma have become very fragile. It seems that the Buddhadharma has a certain life-span. When the Dharma moved to Tibet, Buddhism came to an end in India. Now, it seems that the life of the Dharma is almost finishing in Tibet, and is moving to the West. Guru Rinpoche said that during the future degenerate times, Buddha's doctrine in Tibet will become like a handful of beans you can throw on the floor. They fly in every direction but they never stay in one place. It's interesting

Lama Tharchin Rinpoche, Los Angeles, 1994; while in America, he established the Vajrayana Foundation and the retreat center, Pema Ösel Ling.

that the communists had the idea that they will finish the story of Dharma in Tibet. But the result has been that they have sent it out into the whole world.

When the Dharma was coming to Tibet, many scholars, Buddhas, master teachers were reborn in Tibet, preparing to bring Dharma into Tibet. Now Tibetan Buddhism is again moving to the West. I have met many people who have memories and past lifetimes in Tibet. Different culture, different body but the mind's habit is the same, they care about it so much and they have ability.

Due to skillful means, according to people's mental capacity, Buddha Shakyamuni taught 84,000 different levels of teachings. Art is a very powerful tool to introduce the ultimate true nature of wisdom. Tibetan art is unique. There are two different styles for artists, there is art you copy that depends on external things like a mountain, a lake, a waterfall, people. But Tibetan Dharma art is the other way. It has rules—perfect Buddha body, *bodhisattva* body, deity body, each has proportions that never change. Color has rules. The basic five colors represent the five wisdoms. The art never changes because the knowledge has self-standing rules. Individuals cannot make it up. Master beings and Mahasiddhas have visions. There is a perfect way to arrange mandalas, statues, stupas, symbols of Buddha's wisdom.

The Buddha himself said, "during the degenerate time, anyone thinks of me, I will be right in front of him," because Buddha's emanations are unobstructed. In this time of high technology, there are many ways to preserve this culture—videos, cameras. In Tibetan education, you have to learn and memorize and pass a test. In one way it's hard, but in another way I really appreciate what we learn. If it was on a tape that the Chinese took, I wouldn't have it in my mind. When you look at the expression of enlightened beings, you can get that taste in your mind.

Q: Westerners are very hungry to learn, but what about the young generation of Tibetans?
A: I have that concern too. We don't have that vital part of older lama to younger tulkus, passing lineages; it is very weak. My biggest fear is that soon we won't have wonderful realized and experienced teachers. Younger lamas are more interested in modern culture. But I have seen these young lamas, tulkus. They are amazing so then I have a little confidence. I also have faith in what Guru Rinpoche said, "My doctrine will never disappear." In Tibet, the king Lang Darma tried to destroy sutrayana, tantrayana, but he didn't do it. Mao didn't do it either.

Young Tibetan kids are mostly interested in worldly education; a lot of Western people are interested in Dharma. That's why I'm saying that Dharma as a doctrine is moving to the West.

Q: It's almost like among Tibetans, young people don't feel cool to be studying Dharma. I'm puzzled by it. They have some faith of course, and they'll go to see His Holiness the Dalai Lama, but to study and sit and learn Dharma, they don't do it.
A: That's okay. Dharma doesn't only belong to Tibetans. It's for any sentient being, anyone who has buddha nature, Dharma is vast, nonsectarian.

HER EMINENCE DAGMO JAMYANG SAKYA

DAGMO WAS BORN IN KHAM, eastern Tibet. The niece of the renowned Sakya master, His Eminence Deshung Rinpoche, Dagmo trained in Buddhism from an early age, studying with many great masters in Tibet. She became the Sakya Dagmo (Holy Mother) of the Sakya lineage when she married Jigdal Dagchen Rinpoche, the head of the Phuntsok Phodrang branch of the Khon dynasty of the Sakya school. Dagmo is considered an emanation of Tara, the female Buddha of compassion. After escaping Tibet, then living in exile in India, and finally settling in Seattle, Washington where she raised a family, she brings to her teachings a special quality of compassion and understanding of life in the West.

Malibu, California, 2003

Q: What's the role of women in Buddhism?
A: In Buddhist teachings, there is no difference between men and women. They're equal. There are male and female bodhisattvas. Because of culture in Tibet and all of Asia, there have been more male than female lamas although there have always been many enlightened beings who are women. Traditionally, woman had more obstacles (to receiving teachings and practicing) because they bear children and take care of the family. Otherwise, there's no difference between women and men on the path to enlightenment.

Q: How has being a mother influenced you?
A: I'm glad I was a mother, and grandmother, when we came to America. In America, nobody feeds you or gives you anything. You have to work so I worked many years. Worker, mother, housewife. I had to go through experiences, not just through sitting and renouncing everything; I'm glad I'm learned that way. Now I can teach my own experiences.

Q: Tara is very special to you. Can you speak about her?
A: When I was four years old, I was introduced to Tara. Although I am from a Sakya family, and was married to a Sakya lama, I received teachings and empowerments from all four sects of Buddhism, particularly Tara teachings and blessings. My root teacher was my maternal uncle. All my life, I have practiced and done the proper Tara retreats, everything that needs to be done; Tara is my main practice.

Q: What are some of Tara's essential qualities?
A: Tara has 21 different manifestations and many names. A Sanskrit name, a Tibetan name. The Chinese call her *Quan Yin*. Tara's quality is vast. In Tibetan Buddhism, Tara is the mother of all buddhas and bodhisattvas. Tara herself says she will take care of all sentient beings like a loving mother. For me, Tara has always been there, all through my life. Tara is my deity and protector.

Q: Why are there different aspects of Tara?
A: In Buddhism, there are different manifestations, all essences of Buddha's emanation; whatever is necessary. People have different practices for different achievements. Green Tara is generally the activity aspect in Buddhism. White Tara is more for longevity, protection, and extending life. Tara is for anybody who wishes to practice. It's good to receive empowerment. With the mind initiation, you can meditate that Tara's mind and your mind are inseparable.

Q: Anything more about the essential qualities of Tara?
A: Tara is like a loving mother. Everybody needs a mother. Without a mother we wouldn't even be here. [A mother] who is caring and loving. When we escaped from Tibet, every day we asked Tara, "Which route do we take? How are we going to go?" We didn't know how to cross the Himalayas. And Tara guided us through.

TULKU THUBTEN RINPOCHE

BORN IN 1968 IN EASTERN TIBET, Tulku Thubten Rinpoche began his formal Buddhist studies at the age of 13. He trained in the Nyingma tradition under Tsurlo Rinpoche at Mahr Do Tashi Ghakyil Monastery. At 15, Tulku Thubten was recognized as the incarnation of Ahnam Lama, a chief disciple of Kunkhyen Dudjom Lingpa. He has been living in the United States since 1992. Besides being a Dzogchen master, Rinpoche is an accomplished calligrapher, poet, astrologer, and translator. Having been raised in the remote Golok region of eastern Tibet, he was able to train with some of the few great masters who managed to survive the worst years of the Chinese persecution. Rinpoche's mastery of English and his effort to educate himself about Western culture has enhanced his unique and accessible method of teaching. He gives hope for this spiritual tradition that has lost so many of its great masters.

Q: Where are you from?
A: I'm from Eastern Tibet, Golok.

Q: You were recognized as an incarnated lama.
A: Yes, I was recognized at age fifteen as an incarnation of a great yogi from Golok who was known as Ahnam Lama. He was a *Mahasiddha,* meaning someone who demonstrates miraculous powers as a sign of their achievement. He passed away a long time ago, even before the Chinese came. When I was recognized, I thought that was like putting a royal crown on a beggar. Nowadays, I don't pay attention to those types of recognitions. Recognized or not, it doesn't make much difference if you are arrogant and uncompassionate. If you are compassionate toward all beings and not self-centered, then you are holy. In the old days, they had a pure, authentic tradition of recognizing lamas without political agendas. People often mistake charisma for spiritual realization. There are so many truly sublime beings incognito that we never recognize.

Q: What is the recent history of your monastery?
A: During the Chinese invasion in Tibet, in the late 1950s, my monastery was devastated and then completely destroyed during the Cultural Revolution. In the late 1970s, there was a change in Chinese politics giving limited freedom to Tibetans to preserve their culture and religion so we were able to restore our monasteries. Most lamas in my monastery died through illness, being killed, or in the concentration camp. One of our few great surviving lamas was my personal teacher, Lama Tsurlo.

Q: How can Tibetan culture and religion, the Buddhist way of life, be preserved?
A: We can preserve Tibetan culture and especially the spiritual tradition, which is a unique form of Buddhism that is extremely rich and profound, by teaching Tibetan children their language and their religion. The new generation has a responsibility to carry on their lineage, their heritage. The parents, too, have a big responsibility to make sure those opportunities are available and to teach their children.

Q: Who are some of the deities you are close to?
A: I like to practice Dzogchen because it is formless meditation, and in some sense it transcends all methods, analysis, and archetypes. It's simply realizing our true essence on the spot and becoming awakened without waiting for any precise time or place. It's instant realization. At the same time, I have a very strong connection to specific deities. One of my favorites is Tröma, known as Kali in India, which means the wrathful goddess. She is a dark goddess. Since she is the goddess of destruction, her significance is that she destroys one's ego, attachment, obsessions with ideas and concepts, and brings about egoless wisdom. The practice of Kali is very transformative. It is called Chod practice in Tibetan. Kali is really changing my life. I have been teaching Kali practice the last five years and it's been affecting many people in a very experiential way.

The path of Kali is to not escape the chaos and challenges that life brings. You simply accept them as a blessing of Kali and take them into your heart without fear or resistance, learning to recognize that everything is illusion and fundamentally equal . There are no good or bad circumstances.

Venice, California, 2003

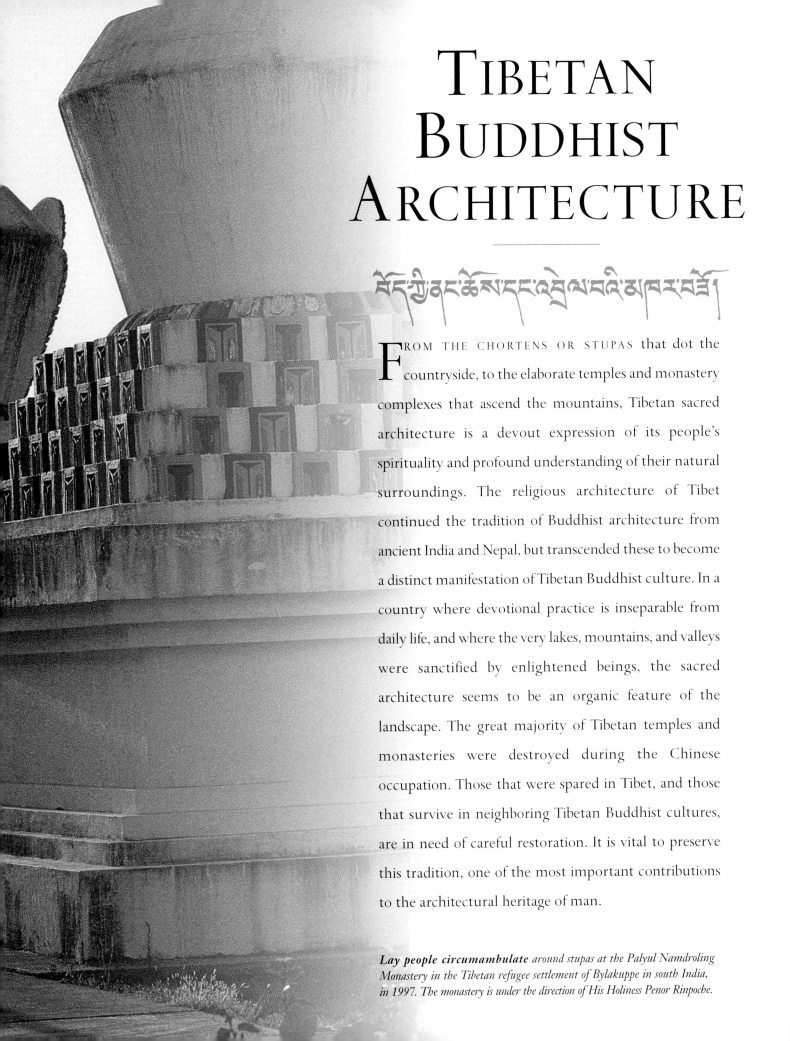

TIBETAN BUDDHIST ARCHITECTURE

བོད་ཀྱི་ནང་ཆོས་དང་འབྲེལ་བའི་མཁར་རྩིག

FROM THE CHORTENS OR STUPAS that dot the countryside, to the elaborate temples and monastery complexes that ascend the mountains, Tibetan sacred architecture is a devout expression of its people's spirituality and profound understanding of their natural surroundings. The religious architecture of Tibet continued the tradition of Buddhist architecture from ancient India and Nepal, but transcended these to become a distinct manifestation of Tibetan Buddhist culture. In a country where devotional practice is inseparable from daily life, and where the very lakes, mountains, and valleys were sanctified by enlightened beings, the sacred architecture seems to be an organic feature of the landscape. The great majority of Tibetan temples and monasteries were destroyed during the Chinese occupation. Those that were spared in Tibet, and those that survive in neighboring Tibetan Buddhist cultures, are in need of careful restoration. It is vital to preserve this tradition, one of the most important contributions to the architectural heritage of man.

Lay people circumambulate around stupas at the Palyul Namdroling Monastery in the Tibetan refugee settlement of Bylakuppe in south India, in 1997. The monastery is under the direction of His Holiness Penor Rinpoche.

STUPAS: SACRED STRUCTURES

STUPAS ARE ARCHITECTURAL REPRESENTATIONS of the Buddha's body, speech, and mind, and every detail of their construction contains a vast and multilayered symbolism that make them a blueprint for enlightenment. Stupas (called *chortens* in Tibet) range in size from small devotional statues to altarpieces to grand monuments, such as the Great Stupa at Bodghaya, India, and contain holy relics, texts, and ritual objects. Buddhists of all traditions are often seen circumambulating stupas to keep the aspiration for enlightenment at the center of their awareness. Though the word *stupa* is said to derive from the Sanskrit root *stu,* meaning "to worship" or "to praise," the practice of creating stupa-like structures has existed from neolithic times when burial mounds or cairns were constructed as reliquaries for the remains of holy people. The remains of great leaders of pre-Buddhist and early Buddhist India were enshrined in simple monuments that have not survived, but one of the earliest existing stupas is the one at Sanchi, India, built in the 2nd century BC. The basic structure is a circle in a square (the basis of most religious architecture, from the pyramids to gothic cathedrals), but Buddhist stupa architecture, exists in its own plane, transcending the influences of architecture past and present. Stupa design consists of a square base surmounted by a dome crowned with a spire of thirteen tapering steps, a lotus shape, and a sun supported by a crescent moon. These five geometric shapes correspond to the elements of earth, water, fire, air, and space, which, in their purified form, symbolize the body and mind of a Buddha; the overall form is said to be that of the Buddha seated in meditation. It is believed that the power of actions performed near a stupa is greatly magnified and can create great stores of merit or positive energy that can travel through lifetimes, even if those actions are accidental.

DESIGN FOR ENLIGHTENMENT

It was not for personal honor, but to inspire others to follow the spiritual path, that prompted Shakyamuni Buddha to give his followers special instructions on the design of the structure that would contain his relics. After Buddha's death, it is said that his ashes and bones were divided among the princes of eight kingdoms. A stupa was built

A line of chortens in the Zanskar Valley of Ladakh, with the peaks of the Himalayas in the distance, 1997.

in each kingdom to symbolize one of the eight major events in the Buddha's life: birth, enlightenment, giving teachings, descending from the heavenly realm, performing miracles, reconciling disagreements in the monastic community, voluntarily prolonging his life, and entering the final great nirvana or liberation. All eight models were incorporated in Tibet, where the design and construction of stupas reached a zenith and became an integral part of spiritual life. Some of the oldest stupas in Tibet were built at Samye, the first Tibetan monastery, established in the 8th century by Padmasambhava.

KUMBUM STUPA

Kumbum in Tibetan means "hundred thousand Buddha images." The Great Chorten at Palkhor Choide

Monastery at Gyantse, built in 1560-77, is one of Tibet's two intact examples of a Kumbum stupa and considered a great achievement of Tibetan architecture. A perfect three-dimensional mandala, its stepped tiers are filled with over 75 chapels, visited by pilgrims as they ascend in the levels in a clockwise circumambulation. The interior is adorned with magnificent frescoes that are a rare and extensive visual chronicle of Indian and Tibetan Buddhism. Eyes are painted on all four sides of the lowest square level—a Nepalese tradition—and represent those of the Buddha.

The Great Chorten, left, a Kumbum stupa at Palkhor Choide Monastery, in Gyantse, Tibet; only several hundred monks remain from its peak of 5,000 before 1959.

*Following pages, **the brilliant orange** and red exterior of the Dzongsar Institute; built in Himachal Pradesh, India in 1985.*

STUPA CONSTRUCTION TODAY

Bodhi Stupa consecration ceremony

Stupas, once a common sight in the Tibetan landscape, were mostly destroyed after the Chinese invasion in 1959. Today, however, stupas are being erected by Tibetan Buddhists in many countries around the world, such as the Bodhi Stupa at the Kagyu Shenpen Kunchab Dharma Center, in Santa Fe, New Mexico (right), which was consecrated in 1986 by the late Kalu Rinpoche, Chagdud Tulku Rinpoche, and other Tibetan and western lamas (left). Buddha prophesied that in the future, the repair and construction of stupas would protect humanity from negative forces during dangerous and troubled times. He also taught that building a stupa creates the causes for being affluent, healthy, influential, and spiritually inclined in one's future life. Stupas are believed to bring prosperity and

harmony to the surrounding communities, and to prevent natural disasters by pacifying harmful environmental forces. At the consecration, lamas perform a ceremony to invite enlightened beings to imbue the stupa with their presence. Sacred objects and relics of Buddhist masters are then placed inside to amplify its enlightened power. In Tibetan Buddhism especially, it is customary to build a stupa when a great teacher dies, since even after cremation the remains of a guru are regarded as sacred. The stupa embodies the teacher's awakened mind, and so becomes a place where students can connect with his or her essential wisdom.

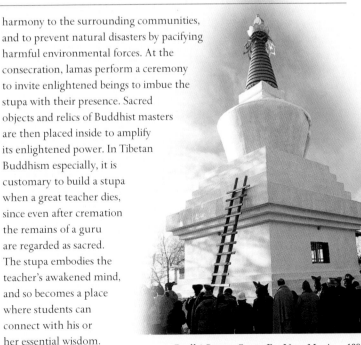

Bodhi Stupa, Sante Fe, New Mexico, 1986

MONASTERIES

Built over 600 years *ago in Leh, India, the Gelupka Thiksey Monastery, above, has twelve ascending levels and houses a 50-foot-tall (15 m) Buddha statue, the largest in Ladakh, commissioned by the Dalai Lama to commemorate his 1980 visit.*

The dramatic vista *as seen from Sera Monastery, left, which was founded in 1419 by Sakya Yeshe, a disciple of Tsongkhapa, founder of the Gelug sect. Until the Chinese invasion of 1959, Sera had a monastic population of several thousand; only several hundred remain today.*

A dramatic aerial view *of the great Ganden Monastery, below, shows the reconstructed buildings in the center, among the ruins. Ganden was established in 1417 by Tsongkhapa as the first Gelugpa monastery; it was destroyed by the Chinese in 1966 during the Cultural Revolution.*

O F THE ORIGINAL TIBETAN MONASTERIES, which numbered over 6,000 at one time, as few as fifty survived the Chinese invasion. However, many of the original monasteries, such as the great monastic universities of Ganden, Sera, and Drepung, have been reconstructed in exile in India and Nepal. These impressive structures with looming white-washed walls that literally rise out of the mountains, are designed to remind one of the value and sanctity of the Buddha's teachings which they house—both in the texts that are studied, as well as in the minds of the monastic community itself. Tibetan scholars believe that some of the first monasteries were established by groups of nomadic monks who eventually settled on land that was donated to them by rich landowners or local aristocrats. The layouts of Tibetan monasteries are based on the design of Tibetan royal palaces. Religious symbols are affixed to the roofs, and the huge doors are brightly colored, with highly ornate gold fixtures. Every detail has spiritual significance including the choice of colors, which are the same as those used in traditional Tibetan homes. Blue, green, red, white, and yellow represent the five elements and are considered auspicious.

MONASTERY DESIGN

Monasteries have similar floor plans to those of Tibetan noble houses, although monastic buildings are typically much larger in scale and more elaborately designed. The basic layout of Tibetan monasteries is largely the same, a model inspired from Buddhist India. They were constructed in traditional Tibetan style with exterior stone and earth walls and an interior cross-pattern of posts and beams, by generations of master builders who passed on their skills from father to son. Monasteries were built as centers of learning, and their elements are designed to teach and inspire. The architecture is simultaneously pragmatic and deeply symbolic. A number of monasteries were built in the shape of a mandala—the celestial abode of an enlightened being—with a square central hall and four colleges placed at each cardinal direction, all enclosed within a circular wall. In a typical Tibetan monastery, the quantity and size of windows increase with each floor as the white-washed walls, massive at the base, taper inward and become thinner towards the higher stories. From the debate courtyard, a number of steps lead through large imposing doors to the main hall, which can be several stories high. This is the heart of the monastery, where the monks gather for daily prayers and special ceremonies. On the second floor of the hall there is generally a room reserved for visiting high lamas. There is also another room built exclusively to receive the Dalai Lama. In monasteries throughout Tibet, these rooms were meticulously prepared and maintained, in the event that the monastic community was blessed by a visit from their spiritual leader—a tradition that continues in exile. If the Dalai Lama ever uses the room, even for a few hours, it becomes a shrine from that time onwards, and a place where people visit to receive blessings. Inside the main hall, thangkas and murals of teachers and enlightened beings gaze down from the walls, and colorful silk banners and brocades hang from the ceiling. The columns and capitals are the most decorated parts of the hall, and are often covered with carved motifs painted in the five colors: yellow, green, red, white, and blue, which are found throughout Tibetan art and culture. The prayer wheel house is actually a single room that is almost entirely filled by a huge central prayer wheel and small altar, with an anteroom where the caretaker monks reside. Tibet is currently undergoing a rebuilding effort to repair the destruction inflicted in the 1950s and '60s, but many renovations are being done with concrete instead of wood, which changes the structure's traditional character.

A traditional Tibetan monastery door handle is made of brightly colored fabric and tied onto an ornate knocker, such as this one in Ladakh, India, 1997.

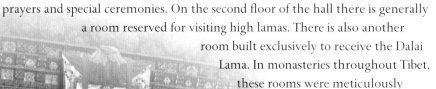

Monks at the Nyingma Monastery in Himachal Pradesh, India, take part in a ceremony in the main hall of the monastery, 1997, such halls typically reach three stories from floor to ceiling.

A monk prays in the sunlit interior of the sacred Jokhang temple, in Lhasa, 1990, right. Built in the 7th century AD, the temple interior contains among the oldest architectural woodcarvings in the world still in existence; almost every wooden surface—columns, beams, doors, window frames—is intricately carved with botanical or figurative designs illustrating Tibetan mythology.

POTALA PALACE

P ERCHED ON TOP OF THE TOWERING RED HILL
that rises above the city of Lhasa is the majestic Potala
Palace, one of the masterpieces of world architecture.
Located at 12,000 feet (3,700 m) above sea level—the
loftiest palace ever built—this imposing thirteen-story
monument was the political and religious heart of Tibet:
the seat of the Tibetan government, the winter home to
generations of Dalai Lamas, a center of Buddhist learning
and training, and still one of the holiest pilgrimage sites
for Tibetan Buddhists.

BUILDING AN ARCHITECTURAL WONDER

The city of Lhasa, which means "Place of the Gods" in Tibetan, was
established c. AD 633 by King Songtsen Gampo, who built a citadel on
the site of the current Potala. This early palace was destroyed by fire,
but two small chapels are said to have survived and were incorporated
into the Potala Palace, the epic project initiated in c. 1645 by the Fifth
Dalai Lama. It took approximately eight years and thousands of
workers, artists, and craftsmen to build the White Palace, the immense
structure that forms the outer perimeter of the Potala. The Fifth
Dalai Lama died in 1682 and did not live to see it completed. It is said
that he asked for news of his death to be withheld from the public

The sheer façade of the Potala Palace
rises dramatically out of the Red Hill, below.
The palace is constructed of wood, stone, and earth,
and was built without the use of nails or steel.

in order not to impede completion of the central Red Palace, which was built between 1690–1694. It is an engineering feat rising 383 feet (117 m) high, with over 1,000 rooms and untold numbers of statues, shrines, and paintings. Workers dug up the earth from the hill behind the palace, creating a deep crater that was made into a lake; in the center of the lake the Fifth Dalai Lama built a temple filled with sacred murals that he and subsequent Dalai Lamas used for personal meditation. The Thirteenth Dalai Lama extended the Potala in the early 1920s, renovating many rooms and adding two stories to the Red Palace.

A SYMBOLIC RESIDENCE

The White Palace served as the living quarters and offices for the Dalai Lama and his large staff; it became the Dalai Lamas' winter residence beginning with the Seventh Dalai Lama (1708–55) (the Dalai Lama's summer home, Norbulingka, was built c. 1740). The Red Palace houses shrines, temples, and a memorial hall with eight elaborate gold funerary stupas for the Fifth to the Thirteenth Dalai Lamas, excluding the Sixth. The Western wing of the Potala housed the Namgyal Monastery, the Dalai Lamas' private monastery. In 1994, the Chinese completed a five-year $80 million-dollar renovation of the Potala to prevent structural damage, and reopened it as a museum; critics maintain that in doing so they have diminished the Potala's status as a Tibetan cultural symbol and have turned it into a source of revenue for the Chinese tourist industry.

The soaring columns of the
Chanting Hall in the Potala Palace, right.
The interior of the Potala contains
the largest expanse of classic Tibetan
woodcarving to be found in the country.

MONASTIC LIFE

དགོན་པའི་ནང་གི་མི་ཚོ།

BEFORE THE CHINESE INVASION OF TIBET, there were half a million monks and nuns living in monasteries and nunneries around the country, making up about ten percent of the entire population. Almost every family had a son or daughter who was ordained. Laypeople traditionally provided material support to the monastic community, relying on them in return to give guidance, advice, and inspiration, as well as to perform rituals and blessings. Almost 200 monasteries and nunneries have now been reestablished in India and Nepal with a population of 18,000. The number of monks has more than doubled in exile since 1980, and the population of nuns has increased even more dramatically, though nuns still make up less than five percent of the overall monastic population. Monks and nuns are having to work even harder in exile to raise the necessary funds to run the monasteries and nunneries, as there are fewer traditional avenues of support. The life of a Tibetan monastic is often rigorous, requiring great dedication and discipline. The Buddhist monastic tradition establishes ethics and morality as foundations for the spiritual life.

Monks in prayer at Dzongsar Institute in Himachal Pradesh, India, 1997. The Institute was founded by Dzongsar Kyentse Rinpoche; a painting of his previous incarnation, the late Jamyang Kheyntse Chokyi Lodro, is displayed on the altar.

ENTERING THE SANGHA

THE LIFESTYLE OF THE *SANGHA* (community of monks and nuns) is very basic, with simple food and few personal possessions. The maroon and yellow patchwork robes and shaved heads symbolize renunciation of attachment to external appearances and ordinary comforts. Celibacy is essential, and in fact, the vows and precepts of monks and nuns are considered fundamental to their spiritual development. These precepts were described by the Buddha, not to restrict personal freedom but to inspire individuals to attain the ultimate liberation—eternal freedom from suffering for the benefit of all living beings. As in all aspects of Buddhism, proper motivation is essential. The idea behind ordination is to develop a life of contentment, simplicity, and modesty, with few desires or distractions. This is not so that an individual can escape from the stresses and responsibilities of the world, but to develop forbearance, self-discipline, and introspection amidst a conducive and supportive community. Such a life, focused on the study of the Buddhist path, is geared towards bringing about an internal transformation in which universal responsibility replaces familial obligations.

A monk turning a large prayer wheel in Kham Pagar Monastery in Himachal Pradesh, India, 1997.

MONASTIC LIFE IN EXILE

Although much was lost in the years following the Chinese invasion, many texts have been salvaged, and great teachers have survived to pass on their wisdom. In exile, Tibetan monasteries and nunneries are once again becoming not only historical repositories of knowledge

Nuns at Ganden Choeling Nunnery *in Dharamsala, India, take part in a ceremony, 1997.*

Child monks *attend lessons at Ganden Jangtse Buddhist Monastery in Mundgod, south India, 1997.*

but important centers for the present and future transmission of the Buddha's teaching. The reasons that children in exile come to monastic centers go beyond tradition. Refugee families may seek to give their children the standard of education and living conditions that they themselves cannot provide. Many of the children are orphaned or their only family is back in Tibet. As a result, monastic institutions are receiving an increasing number of children and adolescents, and many are expanding their curriculum to meet their educational needs with classes in English, Hindi, math, science, literature, computer training, and social science. Some are even allowing formerly prohibited recreational activities such as football and chess.

At most monastic centers, however, the existing facilities are over-burdened and there is a desperate need for teachers, classrooms, and textbooks. Although most monasteries try to supplement donations and sponsorships through small enterprises such as farming and handicraft centers, they are still barely self-supporting. In the spirit of altruism, however, the Dalai Lama is encouraging monasteries to engage in more humanitarian projects. At Ganden Monastery, for example, the monks are sharing their donations with the local Indians and are sponsoring a new schoolhouse for the Indian community.

DAILY LIFE OF MONKS & NUNS

Most monasteries observe rigorous but flexible schedules. At Sera Monastery in Bylakuppe, southern India, the only fixed times are for the *pujas* (ritual prayer offerings) and debate sessions. At daybreak, a gong summons monks to assemble in the main temple for morning prayers, which consist of two hours of chanting many pages of Tibetan text. A crew of monks serves butter tea several times during the ceremony. After prayers, the monks gather for breakfast in a communal hall before beginning the first debate session, during which they

Monks perform pujas *during a meditation retreat at Palyul Namdroling Nyingmapa Monastery in Bylakuppe, southern India, 1997.*

During the Gelug Monlam *festival held in Dharamsala in 1997, monks rush to bring food that will be served to the other monks taking part in the ceremony.*

learn to sharpen their reasoning skills.
After lunch, monks have free time to nap,
study, or stroll into the nearby village.
Classes resume in the afternoon, with
another prayer session at four o'clock.
Following afternoon prayers, the
evening debate session begins, lasting
over three hours with prayers in
between. After a short rest, most of the
monks return to their rooms to
memorize and recite texts and do
their personal spiritual practice.
Promising students can study for
their geshe degrees, the Tibetan
Buddhist equivalent to a doctorate
of philosophy. The geshe study
program at Sera Monastery lasts
fifteen years, a shorter time
than in Tibet.

A nun sweeps at Tsuk
*Lhakhang Temple, the main
temple in Dharamsala, near the
palace of His Holiness, 1997.*

NUNNERIES

Nunneries in Tibet were traditionally less
structured and had less prestige than the
monasteries, with
fewer resources and
little access to
higher education in
Buddhist studies. In
exile, however, a
new generation of
nuns are now
performing religious
activities formerly

Nuns making tsa tsas, Dharamsala

only done by monks, such as creating sand
mandalas, performing ritual dances, and
engaging in philosophical debate. Nuns are
now learning in the grand tradition of
Tibetan monastic culture. At a nunnery in
Nepal, for example, a number of students
are enrolled in a
twenty-year geshe
degree program,
the first geshe
program ever to
include nuns as well
as monks. In this
way, nuns are
helping to preserve
the Tibetan
Buddhist religion and culture, a task that
His Holiness the Dalai Lama has stated as
being the foremost responsibility of the
Tibetan exiled community.

MONASTIC TRAINING

A NEWLY ORDAINED MONK OR NUN is appointed a
room master who is responsible for their welfare and
orients them to monastic life. Young monks and nuns
begin their studies with basic Tibetan language and
grammar, literature, chanting, and prayers, with the older
monks studying history, philosophy, and analysis and
memorization of classical Buddhist scriptural treatises.
Although there is an emphasis on scholarship, sacred arts,
astrology, and medicine are also taught.

THE ART OF DEBATE
The Buddha declared "Just like examining gold in order to know
its quality, you should put my words to the test. Do not accept
them merely out of respect." The Tibetan Buddhist art of debate,
tsod-pa, has been used through the ages to put the Buddha's words
"to the test" and train practitioners in logical reasoning and critical analysis. In ancient India, and later in Tibet, great religious
debates provided a fresh perspective on the teachings and ensured
that only the tenets that could survive profound and repeated
scrutiny endured. Monastic debate resembles a lively combination

Monks at Ganden Shartse Monastery in Mundgod, southern India, perfect their skills in the art of making sand mandalas, 1997.

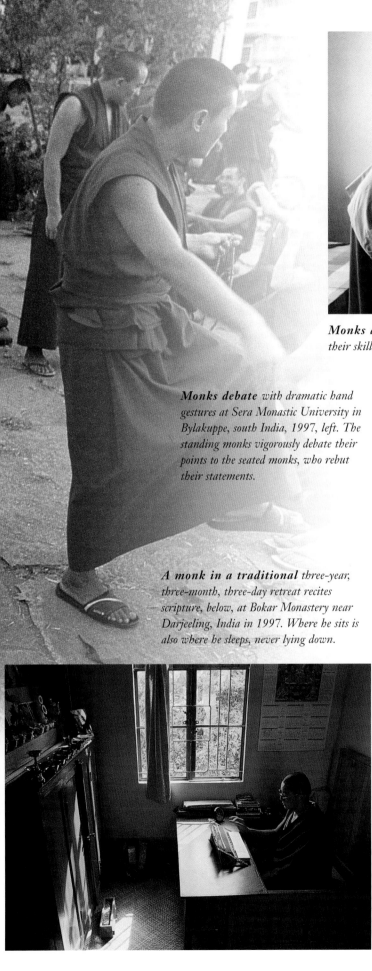

Monks debate with dramatic hand gestures at Sera Monastic University in Bylakuppe, south India, 1997, left. The standing monks vigorously debate their points to the seated monks, who rebut their statements.

A monk in a traditional three-year, three-month, three-day retreat recites scripture, below, at Bokar Monastery near Darjeeling, India in 1997. Where he sits is also where he sleeps, never lying down.

of a courtroom cross-examination and a martial art. However, its purpose is to hone skills in logical reasoning, memory, concentration, and inventiveness, and to ensure that subjects are not just learned by rote but are fully grasped and understood on many levels.

Once or twice a day, monks gather in the monastery courtyard to test their knowledge in debate. The sessions often break up into small informal groups that can continue late into the evening. The monks break up into pairs. One monk strikes an imposing stance before another who is seated and loudly challenges him to a philosophical duel. The seated monk then retorts with his own counterarguments to the statements his opponent has made. The debating arena is not for the faint-hearted. The scene is boisterous, creating a challenging environment for concentration. In employing the full attention of the debater in body, speech, and mind—through dramatic hand gestures and body movements, fast and prolific discussion, and logical analysis—the topic is learned on many levels. Each hand gesture has a specific meaning. The back of the right hand slapping into the palm of the left, for example, is akin to an exclamation mark, indicating when the questioner has made his point. The defender must be able to remain unflustered and respond succinctly and without hesitation, while the challenger tries his best to trump his opponent. Those defeated must then concede to the philosophical position of the victor. If other monks think they can do better, they may jump in and take over one of the positions. The art of debate is particularly stressed in the Gelug school, where it is also a method of student examination. Monks who excel in debate are sent to participate in the Great Prayer Festival debates of Monlam. A Lharam Geshe Degree, the highest degree in Tibetan Buddhism, is conferred on those who win.

SACRED MUSIC

O F TIBET'S UNIQUE MUSICAL TRADITION, none is more distinctive than the vocal and instrumental style of the monastic community. The origin of sacred music in Buddhism began when 500 of the Buddha's disciples sang a song of praise and appreciation on the occasion of his passing away. Sacred music was later developed in Tibet as a tantric meditational art. Tibetan overtone or harmonic chanting, in which monks are able to resonate notes sympathetically while they sing, has caused great interest among ethnomusicologists. All Tibetan monasteries prior to 1959 had their own chanting styles, but the harmonic overtone technique has been especially cultivated by the monks of Gyuto Tantric University. After many years of vocal training, each monk is able to produce a note in three octaves simultaneously.

Previous pages; **monks chant sacred texts** *and play an array of traditional Tibetan musical instruments during a ceremony; Palyul Chokor Ling Nyingmapa Monastery, Himachal Pradesh, India, 1997.*

Monks perform sacred music, *below, during the funeral of Kalu Rinpoche at Sonada Monastery near Darjeeling, India, in 1989.*

Geshe Lobsang Dhonyo, *an* umdze *(chant master) and other monks from Ganden Shartse Monastery, south India, chant sacred music at a ceremony in the Thubten Dharge Ling Monastery, Long Beach, while on tour in California, 1998.*

The resulting sound is almost like an elongated growl, and has been compared to a didgeridoo, the traditional instrument of the indigenous people of Australia. The chanted recitations of the Buddha's teaching, and the deep vocal vibrations and orchestral accompaniment are said to be linked to the movement of energy in the mind and body, and can act to remove physical and psychological impurities. Chanting is led by an *umdze,* or chant master, who must know the entire liturgy by heart (which can be over 200 pages), as well as set the appropriate pace for the ceremony.

SACRED INSTRUMENTS

Traditional temple instruments include cymbals, bells, drums, long horns, and various trumpets, some over eight feet (2.5 m) long, and others fashioned from conch shells. The orchestral arrangements are highly complex, with alternately calm and strident phases, which occasionally dissolve into silence. No aspect of the ceremony is without meaning. The hand bell or *dril-bu,* for example, which is used in many Tibetan Buddhist rituals, represents wisdom, the perfect understanding of the ultimate nature of phenomena.

Monks at Rumtek Monastery, *Gangtok, Sikkim, play long horns called* dung-chen, *right, 1997.*

Monks play drums *during a ceremony at Rumtek Monastery, the seat of the Karma Kagyu lineage in exile founded by the late 16th Karmapa, who died in 1981. His reincarnation, Urgyen Thinley, the 17th Karmapa (his photograph sits on the throne, center), who miraculously escaped from Tibet to India in 1999, has not been able to visit Rumtek yet, and must stay near Dharamsala, where he is under the protection of the Indian military.*

SACRED DANCE

Important figures in Tibet's history, represented by monks wearing masks, watch the sacred dance at Khampagar Monastery in Himachal Pradesh, India, 1997.

Traditionally in Tibet, whenever a monastery celebrated a spiritual festival, the lay community would gather to observe the monks perform three or four days of sacred music and dance. The subject of the dances vary depending upon the occasion, but all share similar themes, which include protection from harm, the generation of auspicious conditions, the purification of negative forces, and destruction of obstacles, particularly those that hinder spiritual practice. The place where the dance is held is also believed to receive blessings of peace and harmony. Many dances reenact stories connected with events in the life of Shakyamuni Buddha and

Deer dance performed at a Mahakala ceremony, 1997, Sherab Ling Monastery, Himachal Pradesh, India. The climax of the ceremony is the destruction of a small effigy, made of cake or meat, during this dance. The effigy represents the year-long accumulation of negativities to be purified by the power of the deity Mahakala.

other great spiritual masters, but they always depict the struggle between negative and positive forces and the ultimate dominion of good over evil.

ORIGINS OF SACRED DANCE

Sacred or *Vajra* dances originated in India and were passed on through a line of tantric adepts to Tibet and Mongolia where they are known as *cham*. All components of tantric practice are present in these dances. The monks go through a series of intricately choreographed movements accompanied by trumpets, drums, bells and cymbals. However, instead of following the rhythm of the music, it is the movements of the dancers that guide the musicians, like a conductor leading an orchestra.

The monks dress in elaborate costumes to represent demons, yogis, nature spirits, protector deities, and animals such as stags and yaks. The "Black Hat" dancers represent realized adepts, while skeleton costumes are worn to symbolize the death of the illusion of an independent and separate self.

A monk at Khampagar Monastery representing Mahakala, enters the sacred dance space.

THE MEANING & SYMBOLISM OF SACRED DANCE

The sacred *cham* dances date back to the introduction of Buddhism, when Padmasambhava danced to consecrate the ground of Tibet's first monastery at Samye. Since they are part of tantric ritual, these dances were not performed in public until the 17th century. Over the years, new dances have been composed, but all of them include the essential components of Vajrayana practice. They demand a high degree of endurance and concentration. Each dancer must maintain a clear visualization of the deity he is representing and take "divine pride" in feeling that he embodies the deity's qualities. In this way, his movements become expressions of

Monks perform a cham dance in old Tibet

enlightenment and his surroundings become the deity's mandala, or divine abode. Tibetan sacred dance is not a vehicle for self-expression, and in fact, the dance is seen as a display of illusory appearances, viewed from the perspective of the wisdom of emptiness of the self and all phenomena. This is why the best dancers are also often highly realized teachers. In describing the ideal qualities of a dancer, the Fifth Dalai Lama stated that "he should make his robes move like a great garuda bird gliding through the skies, move as though his feet were drawing a lotus on the ground, and move his arms to resemble the beating of an eagle's wings."

THE ART OF THE DANCE

The dancers' movements are at times slow and deliberate and at other times fast and furious. Families of Tibetans sit on picnic blankets and watch from the sidelines. Jesters provide comic relief by playfully chasing children and mimicking the amused crowd. The monks chant and meditate around the clock for days beforehand—the dance's outer display is merely a reflection of these inner states of consciousness. The monks must act out of the compassionate motivation to relieve the suffering of others, and the positive energy that is created by the dance is dedicated to this end. The art of Tibetan sacred dance is particularly renowned in the Kagyu school, where some of the dances have been passed down through the mystical visions of great Tantric masters. Monks from the monasteries of this school perform an annual Mahakala dance and *puja,* considered one of the great monastic events of the Tibetan calendar. Sacred dances are banned in Tibet, except as exhibitions for tourists. In exile, however, elder masters are teaching these dances to a new generation of monks who will hopefully become the vessels for their future transmission.

Monks at Sherab Ling Monastery *perform a Mahakala dance, part of a week-long ceremony. This is an important event in the Karma Kagyu tradition, whose practitioners see the protector, Mahakala, as being inseparable from the Karmapa. Himachal Pradesh. 1997.*

With extraordinary precision, *and seeming to literally glide through the air, monks at Rumtek Monastery in Gangtok, Sikkim, do sacred dances during the Tsepchu festival for Padmasambhava in 1997.*

The Mahakala dance *is performed on the last day of the puja and lasts all day. This dance is believed to increase good fortune and subjugate negative forces. Himachal Pradesh, 1997.*

SPIRITUAL PRACTICE

ཆོས་ཀྱི་ཉམས་ལེན །

Within Tibetan Buddhism, there is a broad range of spiritual practices, but all are aimed at transforming the afflicted and ordinary mind into the pure and omniscient mind of a Buddha. Tibetan Buddhists hold that the perception of a separate and independent self, and the attitude of self-cherishing it inspires, lie at the root of all suffering. Therefore practitioners work towards gaining insight into the ultimate nature of reality and learn to cherish others more than themselves. Practitioners adhere to a rigorous ethical code, thus creating positive karma that can ripen into spiritual understanding. Underlying all spiritual practice is the altruistic motivation to attain enlightenment for the benefit of all sentient beings. This extraordinary attitude entails a vow to continue to take rebirth in the world until all beings are liberated from suffering. There is nothing quick about this effort. Rather, one makes a commitment to the path far beyond this lifetime, firmly rooted in the Three Jewels: the Buddha, his teachings or the Dharma, and the spiritual guides or Sangha.

A monk lights butter lamps during the Nyingma Monlam for World Peace at Bodhgaya, India, the place of the Buddha's enlightenment, 1997.

FORMS OF PRACTICE

MOTIVATION

IN THE CONTEXT of Tibetan Buddhism, compassion is not defined as pity, but as the aspiration to end the suffering of others, which includes their subtlest mental and emotional afflictions. Tibetan Buddhists believe that all sentient beings have been our kind mothers in another lifetime, even if they presently appear to us as our adversaries. Practitioners work to generate *bodhicitta*, the aspiration to reach enlightenment in order to teach and assist others in their spiritual development. Once a person has generated spontaneous and uncontrived bodhicitta, they have become a *bodhisattva*, which literally means "enlightenment hero."

MEDITATION

In Tibetan, the word for meditation is *gom*, meaning "to become familiar with," as meditators learn to habituate their minds to positive states of awareness. There are two main kinds of meditation in Tibetan Buddhism: single pointed meditation and analyatical meditation. Single point meditation is done to calm and steady the mind so that it can remain focused on a chosen object without becoming distracted. Once the mind is stable, then the practitioner can use their analytical awareness to examine the subject at hand, like focusing a microscope to study a slide. For example, a meditator might concentrate on a specific practice aimed at developing compassion. Even the most advanced tantric practices are grounded in love and compassion, and practitioners employ numerous techniques to cultivate these qualities. Tibetan Buddhism also incorporates physical activities into the spiritual path, such as circumambulating holy places and making prostrations to purify the body as well as the mind.

A Bhutanese mother and her daughter, who made a pilgrimage to Bodhgaya, India, prostrate themselves before the Mahabodhi Stupa, 1997.

MANTRAS

Mantras are used so extensively in Tibetan Buddhist practice that the tantric vehicle is sometimes called *Mantrayana*. Mantra channels the mind's tendency for discursive chatter into a spiritual language, which if recited with profound understanding, can invoke the enlightened mind and speech of a buddha. Mantras do not translate into easily understandable phrases, but are multifaceted expressions of enlightened awareness. *Om Mani Padme Hum* is the mantra of Avalokiteshvara, the embodiment of universal compassion. Most Tibetan children know this mantra, called *mani*, even before they can walk, and it is said to encapsulate the entire path to enlightenment within its syllables. Strings of prayer beads, called *malas*, are used to keep track of the number of recitations, and Tibetans can often be seen repeating the mantra and counting on their malas as they go about their daily routine.

At the request of an elderly *widowed Tibetan woman, a group of monks from the Sakya monastery in Himachal Pradesh came to her house to recite prayers for her husband who had died a few years earlier, 1997.*

Mantras are written *on rolled paper and inserted into prayer wheels that are turned clockwise with the help of a weighted ball. While they turn the wheel, a person focuses on spreading the blessings of the mantra throughout the universe. Here, a group of Tibetans taking part in a retreat at Palyul Namdroling Nyingmapa Monastery in Bylakuppe, south India, practice* mani *as they walk.*

PUJAS

Puja is Sanskrit for "offering," and in Tibetan Buddhism, a puja is a ceremony in which offerings are made to holy beings. Vajrayana ceremonies cannot be understood from external appearances alone, as the ritual activities are only outer manifestations of internal mental processes. Offerings are not made for the benefit of the buddhas, but to purify negativity and develop a giving attitude and positive energy in the heart of the practitioner. A special kind of puja in the Tibetan Buddhist tradition is the feast offering of *tsog*, which takes place twice a month. Tsog means "assembly," and refers to the gathering of offerings, as well as to the congregation of practitioners who chant and meditate on Buddhist texts, which outline the path to enlightenment. Offerings of food are made to tantric masters who are visualized as being

inseparable from enlightened beings. Such group practices in the presence of the teacher provide a highly charged and inspirational atmosphere. In the monasteries, the power of a group puja to elicit spiritual understanding is likened to a broom. It is very difficult to sweep with a single piece of straw, but when many pieces of straw are gathered together, then one can clean away the dust.

*A **monk attends to tormas** and food spread out on a table as* tsog *offerings, left during the Nyingma Monlam at the Mahabodhi Stupa in Bodhgaya in 1997.*

*Following pages; **elder Tibetans turn** a large prayer wheel at Palyul Chokor Ling Monastery in Himachal Pradesh, 1997*

*A **Tibetan woman** performing a mandala offering at a Kalachakra Initiation in Siliguri, India, left, 1997. This hand gesture (mudra) represents the entire universe and its contents, which is visualized and offered to enlightened beings.*

***These masters performing** mudras at the Nyingma Monlam at Bodhgaya, India, in 1997, above, are* ngakpas, *yogis who are said to be incarnate masters.*

THE PRACTICE OF VAJRAYANA

Known by Tibetan Buddhists as Vajrayana, tantric practice involves advanced techniques of meditation that harness the forces of human imagination and the body's natural energy centers. These practices are considered to be a highly effective tool that can accelerate our ability to overcome negative states of mind. To successfully engage in tantra, practitioners need to develop certain qualities, such as compassion, meditative concentration, and at least a good intellectual understanding of emptiness—the lack of separate and inherent existence of self and phenomena. After receiving instructions from a teacher in the form of an "empowerment," they learn to visualize themselves as the

*A **Tibetan woman** made pilgrimage to the Mahabodhi Stupa at Bodhgaya, India, 1997, below.*

IMAGES OF ENLIGHTENMENT

Statue of Avalokiteshvara, the Buddha of Compassion

Painting of White Tara

Two central deities of Tibetan Buddhism are Avalokiteshvara (Chenrezig) and Tara. Chenrezig is the embodiment of the compassion of all the buddhas and the patron deity of Tibet. One of his forms has eleven faces and 1,000 arms, symbolizing his ability to see into the hearts of all beings and lead them out of suffering. His front two hands hold a wish-fulfilling jewel, symbolizing his altruistic motivation. In his next right hand, he holds a crystal rosary symbolizing his ability to liberate with skillful means. The blue flower in his left hand represents his compassion. Tara is said to have emerged from the compassionate tears of Chenrezig. She is the embodiment of the buddhas' enlightened activity, and manifests in many forms.

deity and their environment as a sacred realm, while generating the deity's enlightened qualities within themselves. Practitioners utilize sacred art as a tool for visualization. For the unprepared, these practices are ineffectual and can even be harmful, so great importance is placed on learning from qualified spiritual teachers. The secrecy surrounding tantric practice is to avoid misunderstandings about the symbolism, and to protect us from projecting our's delusions and misconceptions onto these practices. For example, wrathful deities may look like monsters, but they are actually compassionate beings who embody the force sometimes required to break through mental and emotional blocks that keep us from realizing our positive potential. The buddhas manifest in many different forms, but all buddhas share the same ultimate nature of perfect compassion and wisdom.

A Tibetan monk does his spiritual practice, right, in a quiet spot by the Mahabodhi Stupa at Bodhgaya, 1997.

KALACHAKRA INITIATION

THE TANTRIC EMPOWERMENT of Kalachakra is associated with world peace and the uniting of diverse forces. It is said to aid in reducing suffering and conflict while increasing loving kindness, compassion, and happiness in the recipients as well as in the environment where it is given. One of the main themes of the Kalachakra is the parallel between the physical world, the human body, and tantra. *Kalachakra* is Sanskrit for "cycles of time." Although there are many complex levels of symbolism, these cycles can be broadly defined as external, internal, and alternative. There are the external cycles of the universe, such as the physical laws of time and space, astronomical orbits, the changing seasons, the transition of night into day, and the cycles of history. The internal cycles deal with the rhythms of the body and its energy movements, including our ever-changing moods. The alternative cycles refer to the Kalachakra tantra, which presents practices to train the mind so that one can eventually become liberated from the limitations imposed by the first two. The vast Kalachakra literature is a profound source of explanations in areas of Buddhist study such as cosmology, astronomy, and astrology.

His Holiness the 14th Dalai Lama giving the Kalachakra empowerment near Siliguri, India, in 1997. His Holiness has given the Kalachakra empowerment more times than any Dalai Lama in history.

The source of the Kalachakra texts is traced back to Shakyamuni Buddha. It is said that King Suchandra, from the "northern land" of Shambhala, attended the Kalachakra teachings that the Buddha gave in South India before an assembly of enlightened beings. Suchandra, who is believed to be an emanation of Vajrapani, the embodiment of the buddhas' enlightened power, returned to Shambhala, where he constructed a three-dimensional Kalachakra mandala and devoted himself to the practice. Years later, the teachings were passed down to another Shambhala king, Manjushri Yashas, revered as an emanation of the Buddha of Wisdom. This king adapted the Kalachakra texts into an abridged version and offered them to his people in order to unify them against impending invasion. The legend of Shambhala

Four monks working on a Kalachakra mandala in Santa Monica, California, 1989. The blueprint for the mandala is created by dipping string into liquid white chalk. The string is stretched over the mandala platform; when plucked, the chalk falls onto the platform, creating a chalk line.

as a kind of heaven on earth subsequently gave rise to the popular mythical paradise of Shangri-la. Shambhala is said to be perceived only by those whose minds are pure. The Buddha prophesized that those who receive the Kalachakra empowerment will be reborn in its mandala, and most Tibetans try to receive this empowerment at least once, believing that it will ensure a future rebirth in Shambhala. The royal lineage of Shambhala kept the Kalachakra teachings in an unbroken transmission.

The Kalachakra texts did not return to India until the 10th century, and approximately one hundred years later they were brought to Tibet, where several traditions and lineages of these teachings developed. In the 1600s, Tibetan Buddhists brought the Kalachakra tradition to Mongolia, China, and Siberia.

The "sand" in a sand mandala *is actually soft white stone that is ground and dyed. At right, a monk rubs a metal stick against a* chakpu, *or special serrated funnel filled with sand, which allows the sand to pour out in a thin stream onto the mandala; Santa Monica.*

The completed Kalachakra mandala, *in Santa Monica. This astounding creation takes over a weeks to make, but monks train for at least two years to memorize the hundreds of symbols and learn the complex techniques needed to create the mandala. It is believed that viewing a completed mandala is a blessing, which both purifies negativity and generates compassion.*

Monks and nuns on the stage with His Holiness the Dalai Lama, during the 1989 Kalachakra Initiation in Santa Monica. His Holiness sits on a throne next to the thekpu, *a special pavilion that houses the mandala. Over 5,000 people were in the audience.*

SAND MANDALAS

In tantric practice, mandalas are the sacred abodes of meditation deities, and as such are expression of enlightened qualities of mind such as compassion and wisdom. Sand mandalas are created as two-dimensional forms that are viewed from above, but they are actually visualized as three-dimensional multistory structures, which are entered by initiates in meditation.

Practitioners who have received the empowerment from the tantric master can visualize the sacred environment of a mandala to transform the conventional mind into the mind of enlightenment. Sand mandalas can take many days to complete. The mandala artist uses a narrow metal funnel (*chakpu*) rubbed with a metal stick to produce a fine stream of sand with which he "paints" the intricate forms of the mandala. In the Kalachakra Mandala, hundreds of manifestations of aspects of mind and reality that constitute the ultimate wisdom mind of the Kalachakra deity are portrayed within a 6 1/2-foot (2-m) wide circle. The mandala is a pictorial representation of the Kalachakra texts themselves. Within its circumference are Buddhist symbols and representations of deities, humans, animals, and plant forms, astronomical bodies, physical

At the end of the Kalachakra empowerment, His Holiness ritually dismantles the mandala by slicing through the sand, to illustrate the nature of impermanence.

The sand from the dismantled mandala *is swept into sacred vases and poured into a nearby body of water to carry its healing energy, peace, and compassion into the world. Above, His Holiness pours the holy sand into the waters of Marina del Rey, 1989.*

elements, architectural structures, and gardens, with Sanskrit syllables forming the outer ring. After the initiation ceremony is completed, sand mandalas are ritually dismantled as a lesson in impermanence, and in the case of the Kalachakra mandalas, are used as an offering for world peace. The Dalai Lama has said that "one doesn't need to be present at the Kalachakra ceremony in order to receive its benefits."

PRESENTING THE KALACHAKRA

Although it belongs to the most profound and highest class of tantra, there are an increasing number of non-Buddhists who participate in the Kalachakra empowerment, and the teachings are open to anyone who wishes to attend. People of all faiths are welcome to attend the three-day Kalachakra ceremony, and while it is not expected that all in attendance will take tantric vows, observers can still benefit from the positive karma that is generated. Not all of the Dalai Lamas choose to give Kalachakra empowerments. His Holiness the 14th Dalai Lama has given the Kalachakra empowerment more times than any Dalai Lama in history, in locations all over the world. In addition, other great Tibetan Buddhist masters sometimes give the Kalachakra Initiation.

PILGRIMAGE

THE TRADITION OF THE BUDDHIST pilgrimage probably began with practitioners visiting the eight stupas constructed over the Buddha's relics after he had passed away. The earliest sites included the places Shakymuni Buddha lived and taught and these remain sacred to all Buddhist traditions. Other pilgrimage sites in the Himalayas include dwelling places of deities and later Buddhist masters.

MOUNT KAILASH

MOUNT KAILASH is one of the most sacred sites in all of Asia. Venerated by Hindus, Jains, Buddhists, and Bönpos alike, ancient Buddhist cosmography views Mount Kailash as the axis mundi, or central hub of the universe, and is regarded by Tibetan Buddhists as the fortress of the tantric deity, Chakrasamvara, and his consort. For Hindus, the mountain is Mount Meru, the throne of Shiva, one of the three main gods of the Hindu pantheon, while Bönpos believe that Mount Kailash was where the Bön founder, Tonpa Shenrab, alighted from the heavenly realm of Olmo Lung Ring. Mount Kailash is called Kang Rinpoche, or "Precious Mountain," by Tibetan Buddhists. Bönpo call the mountain Yungdrung Gu Tse, "Nine-Story Swastika Mountain." Swastikas are ancient auspicious symbols; the nine swastikas represent the Nine Ways of Bön.

Pilgrims gather together in a camp at the base of Mount Kailash, to rest and take a meal, c. 1995.

A Tibetan Buddhist pilgrim prays before *Mount Kailash, c. 1988.*

THE KORA

Mount Kailash is a majestic, snowy dome rising just over 22,000 feet (6,700 m) above sea level, that towers over the plateau in western Tibet, visible for miles in all directions. Four of the mightiest rivers of South Asia originate here: the Indus, Sutlej, Karnali, and Brahmaputra. These rivers supply most of the groundwater to south and east Asia, magnifying the mountain's secular importance. However, its religious significance is what draws the countless pilgrims. Tibetan peasants, farmers, city dwellers, nomads, children, and the elderly turn prayer wheels, prostrate, and recite the *mani*, the mantra of compassion, while making the 32-mile (50-km) clockwise circuit, or *kora*, of the mountain. Bön is the only religion where practitioners circumambulate in counterclockwise fashion. One circumambulation is believed to purify a whole lifetime of negative karma. The ascending path is wide and well-trodden and can be traveled on foot in two or three days, though devout Buddhists extend the journey into weeks with frequent full-body prostrations. It is considered sacrilegious to actually climb Mount Kailash. The route is decorated with brightly colored mantras painted on stones, and prayer flags flapping in the wind that people leave behind as a symbol of the negativities that they are leaving behind.

A Tibetan Buddhist family on pilgrimage making the kora, *or circumambulation around Mount Kailash, c. 1998.*

POTALA PALACE

THE POTALA PALACE, built on the Red Hill in Lhasa by the Fifth Dalai Lama in the 17th century, has long been a major pilgrimage destination for Tibetan Buddhists. The 7th-century Tibetan king Songtsen Gampo, who built an early fortress on the site (destroyed by fire), is believed to have meditated there in a cave shrine upon his conversion to Buddhism. Along with the Dalai Lamas, Songtsen Gampo is considered an emanation of Avalokiteshvara, the Buddha of Compassion, whose mystical abode was Mount Potala in southern India—hence the name "Potala Palace." In addition to many sacred statues, thangkas, altars, and the holy tombs of eight former Dalai Lamas, the Potala Palace contains the chapels Phakpa Lhakhang and Chogyal Drubphuk. These two structures are the oldest surviving on the hill, and thought to be part of Songtsen Gampo's original shrine.

This rare photograph, *above, shows pilgrims on the circumambulation route, or Lingkhor, around the Potala Palace, 1904. Mani stones are stacked to the right in an outdoor shrine, and the walls are covered with painted religious images and adorned with streamers of prayer flags.*

Modern-day pilgrims *turn prayer wheels, in front of the Potala, top of page, c. 1997*

THE JOKHANG

THE JOKHANG TEMPLE is Tibet's most venerated shrine, sacred to all Tibetan Buddhist schools. Like the Potala Palace, the Jokhang was established by King Songtsen Gampo in the 7th century and expanded during the time of the Fifth Dalai Lama. Almost completely destroyed during the Cultural Revolution, since the 1980s it has undergone reconstruction. Pilgrims arrive from all over Tibet, some even making the journey by prostrating all the way. At the temple, they present white silk scarves called *khatas* and butter lamps as offerings to the enlightened beings.

HOUSE OF THE JOWO

The Jokhang stands at the center of old Lhasa, and houses many invaluable relics. The most precious images are the venerated Jowo Shakyamuni Buddha statue, depicting Buddha as a twelve-year-old; and the Jowo Mikyoe Dorjee, of Buddha as an eight-year-old—both are said to be the only two remaining statues of the Buddha's likeness made during his lifetime. The Jowo Shakyamuni was brought to Tibet from China by Songtsen Gampo's wife, Wen Ch'eng, as part of her dowry; and the Jowo Mikyoe Dorjee was the dowry of his Nepali wife, Bhrikuti Devi. The Jokhang, "House of the Jowo," was built by Princess Bhrikjuti as a shrine for the Jowo Mikyoe Dorjee, and the Jowo Shakyamuni eventually came to be housed there as well. During the

Pilgrims pray *and prostrate themselves at the entrance of the Jokhang Temple in Lhasa, Tibet, c. 1988, above, and 1999, below left.*

Chinese Cultural Revolution, the Jowo Mikyoe was abducted by the Chinese. It was sawed in half; the bejeweled, gold upper half was carted off to China to be stripped and melted down—along with thousands of other priceless artifacts from Tibet—while the bottom half was left behind in Lhasa. In 1982, after much pressure from Tibetan officials and high lamas—and to boost their global public image—the Chinese decided to return many Tibetan religious artifacts to Tibet. Somehow the Jowo Mikyoe survived; a search party of Tibetan officials led by Rinbhur Tulku miraculously discovered the Jowo in the Gu Kung (Old Palace) in Beijing, which was being used as a storehouse for the stolen artifacts. The statue was brought back to Tibet in 1983. The Jowo Mikyoe Dorjee is now rejoined with the Jowo Shakyamuni These statues in the Jokhang, their home for thirteen centuries.

BODHGAYA

Many centuries ago, in what is now the Indian state of Bihar, Prince Siddhartha attained enlightenment while sitting under a banyan tree at Bodhgaya and was given the name Buddha. Bodhgaya has since become a center of pilgrimage for Buddhists from all schools and traditions. The exquisite Mahabodhi Temple, built on the site of Buddha's enlightenment, houses a huge Buddha image and has many stupas. A tree growing on its western side is believed to have descended from the original bodhi (enlightenment) tree beneath which the Buddha sat. While Buddhists come from all over the world to Bodhgaya, this hallowed ground, the holiest place for Buddhism, has been transformed by the presence of Tibetan refugees in India who have made it an extraordinarily alive place of spiritual practice. Tibetans circumambulate around the stupa and prostrate before it with great ferver, or find quiet spots on the grounds to meditate or read scripture.

SARNATH

After his enlightenment at Bodhgaya, the Buddha went to Sarnath near Varanassi. Here, he encountered the five ascetics he had practiced with before his awakening. In Deer Park, the Buddha gave his first teaching, The Four Noble Truths, to these men who became his first disciples, thus setting in motion the Wheel of Dharma. For over 1,500 years, the Buddhist monastic tradition flourished at Deer Park until Muslim armies destroyed Sarnath and its religious sites. The 6th-century Dhamekha Stupa is the only stupa at Sarnath that survived from antiquity.

A Tibetan man prostrates while circumambulating around the Mahabodhi Temple at Bodghaya, the site of Buddha's enlightenment. A temple was originally built on the site by the Indian king Ashoka in the 3rd century AD, and the current structure was completed in the 6th century.

TSO PEMA

AN EXTRAORDINARY EVENT in the life of Padmasambhava, the Indian yogi, took place in Tso Pema, near the city of Mandi. Legend tells that he took the young princess Mandarava as his spiritual consort to the fury of the girl's father, the king of Mandi, who tried to have the yogi burned at the stake. Padmasambhava miraculously transformed the flames into a small lake, and emerged unharmed from a giant lotus in the form of a sixteen-year-old boy. Humbled, the king offered Padmasambhava his entire kingdom and gave his blessing for Mandarava to follow the Dharma. Tso Pema, or "Lake of the Lotus," is home to several monasteries and Tibetans, as well as Himalayan hill-tribe people who practice Tibetan Buddhism and circumambulate around the lake expressing their faith in Padmasambhava.

Buddhist pilgrims toss khatas in devotion to Padmasambhava onto a plant growing in Tso Pema (Lake Rewalsar), near Mandi in northern India, 1997.

Buddhists circumambulate around the 6th-century Dhamekha Stupa at Sarnath, left, near Varanassi, where the Buddha gave his first teaching, 1997.

Following pages, monks prostrate at Bodghaya.

A TEACHING IN ZANSKAR

THE REMOTE REGION OF ZANSKAR near Ladakh, India, can only be reached by road three months out of the year. During this time, a rickety bus makes a breath-taking journey over the 19,000-foot (5,800-m) pass into the Zanskar valley from the town of Kargil in Kashmir, near the Pakistani border. These passes become inaccessible with the first snowfall, though for a few weeks in the depths of winter the more intrepid travelers can make the twelve-day trek over the frozen Zanskar river to trade goods in Ladakh, or return to Zanskar from pilgrimages in India. Within the Zanskar area are some centuries-old Tibetan Buddhist monasteries, which support a small monastic community. In the summer of 1997, the people of this remote region were anticipating a rare visit by His Holiness the Dalai Lama. As the day approached, a steady trail of people from the villages scattered within Zanskar's three river valleys began arriving at the site where the teachings were to be held.

People of the Zanskar valley, *a remote area in northern India, walked great distances, left, to see and receive teachings from His Holiness the Dalai Lama, who visited there in 1997.*

A REVERENT AUDIENCE

Zanskar has a short growing season, and the summer is a very busy time as the locals have barely three months in which to grow and harvest and store the food for the rest of the year. It had been a number of years since the Dalai Lama had been here, and hundreds of people put their work aside to take this precious opportunity to receive blessings and instruction from their spiritual leader. The Dalai Lama had just come from giving teachings in Leh, the capital of Ladakh, and arrived in Zanskar by helicopter. He was accompanied by his younger brother, Ngari Rinpoche, who was hosting the visit. Ngari Rinpoche is the head of a number of monasteries in Zanskar, most of which follow the Gelug school of Tibetan Buddhism. The people set up a primitive encampment of tents, where an international team of voluntary health care and aid workers erected makeshift clinics. The Zanskar people

A monk from a nearby monastery *passed out pieces of tall grass that were blessed by His Holiness the Dalai Lama, as part of his 1997 empowerment in Zanskar.*

His Holiness giving an empowerment to Zanskaris, above. He is sitting on a throne in the temple specially built for his visit to Zanskar. The exterior of the temple is seen in the photograph at left, behind the crowd of Zanskaris receiving His Holiness's teachings.

have very little access to medical facilities. A team of European dentists came as volunteers to pull bad teeth, and a French couple helped to sponsor a school for the youth. The children performed Zanskari dances for those in attendance. The Dalai Lama sat on a throne in a small temple facing the crowd, while families took shelter under shrubs from the intense summer heat. With the snow-capped ring of the Himalayas in the distance, the Dalai Lama began to impart what would be two days of Buddhist teachings to a deeply attentive audience. All generations were represented, and the women wore their finest clothes and elaborate headdresses covered with turquoise, which had been passed on through generations of mothers and daughters. There was an expression of reverence mixed with joy on their faces as the Dalai Lama spoke. After the teachings, hundreds of people circumambulated around the Dalai Lama's temple to receive blessings from his presence. As they did so, a halo appeared around the sun.

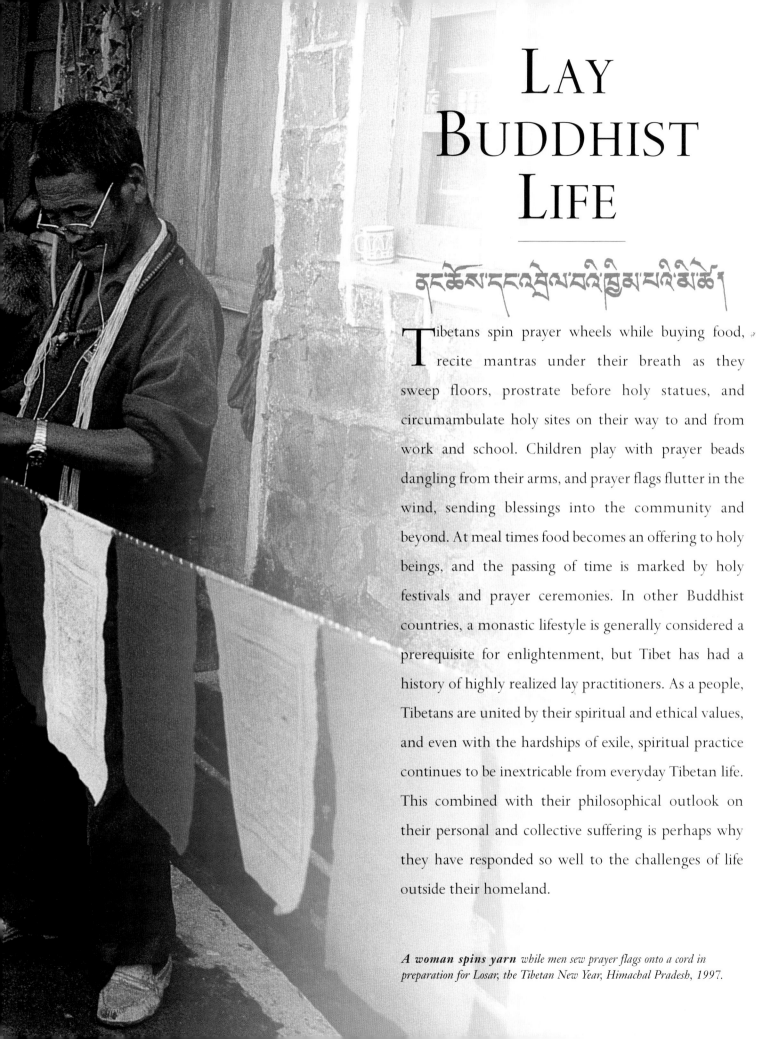

LAY BUDDHIST LIFE

ནང་ཆོས་དང་འབྲེལ་བའི་ཁྱིམ་པའི་མི་ཚེ།

Tibetans spin prayer wheels while buying food, recite mantras under their breath as they sweep floors, prostrate before holy statues, and circumambulate holy sites on their way to and from work and school. Children play with prayer beads dangling from their arms, and prayer flags flutter in the wind, sending blessings into the community and beyond. At meal times food becomes an offering to holy beings, and the passing of time is marked by holy festivals and prayer ceremonies. In other Buddhist countries, a monastic lifestyle is generally considered a prerequisite for enlightenment, but Tibet has had a history of highly realized lay practitioners. As a people, Tibetans are united by their spiritual and ethical values, and even with the hardships of exile, spiritual practice continues to be inextricable from everyday Tibetan life. This combined with their philosophical outlook on their personal and collective suffering is perhaps why they have responded so well to the challenges of life outside their homeland.

A woman spins yarn while men sew prayer flags onto a cord in preparation for Losar, the Tibetan New Year, Himachal Pradesh, 1997.

BUDDHISM AS
A WAY OF LIFE

IN TIBETAN BUDDHISM, LAY PEOPLE are intimately involved in the life of the monasteries, joining the monks and nuns for retreats and empowerments. Although the Buddha's teachings were mostly addressed to monks and nuns, he also gave many discourses to householders. These include a basic code of conduct—not to kill, steal, lie, engage in sexual misconduct, or consume intoxicants. The Tibetan lay population is profoundly religious and spiritual practice is a central, rather than a peripheral activity. The bodhisattva's aspiration to attain enlightenment for the sake of all beings is at the heart of Tibetan Buddhist life and practitioners aspire to maintain this inner motivation. Spiritual awakening is possible to actualize since all beings are said to possess "Buddha Nature"—the seed of enlightenment. With such altruistic motivation, even mundane activities and the responsibilities of family life can become transformed into a path to spiritual realization.

A woman hangs prayer flags outside of her home in Himachal Pradesh, India, in 1997.

PROSTRATION

Prostration is an often misunderstood Buddhist practice. There is no comparison between a Tibetan Buddhist prostrating before a teacher or an image of a Buddha, and a person bowing to an overlord or king. Rather than signifying submission to a religious authority, as it has been interpreted by the communist Chinese government, prostration is a form of meditation on one's own spiritual aspirations and potential. The practitioner touches the hands to the top of the head in a prayer gesture, and then to the throat and heart, symbolizing the enlightened body, speech, and mind respectively. He or she then kneels, placing the forehead on

the floor, and then stands, bringing the hands together overhead before repeating the process. Prostrations are considered a powerful method of purification. The points where the knees, hands and forehead touch the ground constitute the "five disturbing emotions" that are to be overcome—anger, attachment, ignorance, pride, and jealousy. In a full prostration, the practitioner slides all the way out across the floor and brings the arms overhead before rising. A fringe benefit is that prostrations are a good form of aerobic exercise, and many practitioners keep physically fit through this practice.

Bhutanese women who came on pilgrimage to Bodhgaya, the place of the Buddha's enlightenment, prostrate themselves toward the Mahabodhi stupa, 1997.

CELEBRATIONS
WEDDINGS

IN TIBET AND ALSO IN EXILE, arranged marriages are common, but a woman has the right to refuse any offer she is given. While there are also many marriages that are not arranged, young Tibetans, who tend to be shy, prefer to let relatives from the two families discuss the possibility of their marrying. Wedding customs vary from region to region, and often there is no actual ceremony at all, with the man and woman simply forming a verbal agreement to seal their partnership.

A family wedding portrait, Ladakh, early 1900s.

WEDDINGS IN EASTERN TIBET

Traditionally, in Eastern Tibet, after the period of courtship a respected elder is chosen by the groom's family to formally ask the bride's parents for permission for the union to take place. After the girl's maternal uncle approves the match, the two families exchange gifts as a sign of their bond. Money for milk and aprons is presented to the mothers of both families in acknowledgment of their having fed their children with their own milk and worn out many aprons in the process. The families then consult an astrologer to decide on an auspicious date for the wedding. On the eve of the wedding, friends and relatives bid farewell to the son or daughter who is leaving home and moving in with the other family. Representatives from the receiving family welcome the couple and everyone exchanges *khatas*, after

The bride, the groom, and each member of the immediate family receive khatas *(ceremonial scarves) from all of the guests, Himachal Pradesh, 1997.*

which there is singing and dancing. The next morning the groom's uncle begins the wedding ceremony, during which the bride and groom kneel before an altar in the home, and a monk who is close to the family performs a *puja*. Later in the day, family and friends gather in a meeting hall, wearing their best clothes. The bride and groom and their immediate families sit alongside one another, while the guests form a line and places khatas over the heads of everyone in the wedding party. This is followed by a jubilant feast and energetic dancing and singing.

Submerged beneath a wave of white silk, the mother of the groom is covered with khatas, presented to her, and to each member of the wedding party, with wishes for happiness.

A group of women who are friends and relatives of the bride and groom dance in celebration of this auspicious occasion. As they dance, they sing folk songs from Kham, eastern Tibet. The women wear their best traditional Tibetan dresses, called chupas, over long-sleeved silk blouses. Their colorful striped aprons indicate that they are married. Himachal Pradesh, India, 1997.

LOSAR

TIBETAN NEW YEAR OF LOSAR is a major event for Tibetans as well as for other ethnic groups in the Himalayas who practice Tibetan Buddhism, incorporating many aspects of family, social, and spiritual life. The festivities include a number of ceremonies to purify the negativities of the past and prepare for the year ahead. It is believed that one's actions around this time are especially significant, and have a profound effect on the events of the next twelve months. It is considered inauspicious to become angry or upset—special care is taken both individually and communally to avoid negative states of mind, thus ensuring a smooth transition into the new year. Debts are settled and quarrels resolved. Houses and monasteries are given a thorough cleaning and often whitewashed, while old prayer flags and door and window hangings are renewed.

A man fries a batch of khapse *in preparation for Losar. The dough is made from flour and water, and deep fried in yak butter.*

Village women knead dough and roll it into long tubes that will be baked into khapse, *special pastries made especially for Losar.*

NEW YEAR'S EVE, NEW YEAR'S DAY

On New Year's Eve, braided pastries called *khapse* are placed as offerings on altars and given with a silk scarf *(khata)* to visiting friends and relatives. Families dine on thick butter tea and a special soup called *guthuk,* meaning "ninth soup," because it contains at least 9 ingredients. Hidden inside are dumplings filled with various items such as salt, peas, chilies, and even wool or coal, each of which is interpreted in a different way. White ingredients such as salt, for example, are considered propitious. People invite other families and friends to come share a meal or make spontaneous visits—indicating the high esteem that they feel for one another. At the end of the meal, a ceremony is performed to eliminate any residual negative influences. On New Year's Day, everyone puts on their best clothes and goes to the monasteries to give donations and khatas, to

A traditional Losar altar in a Tibetan Buddhist home in India is laden with many ceremonial objects, including candles, incense, small thangkas, and a platter of khapse—*a special braided pastry—which is placed on the altar as an offering to Budhha.*

generate good karma for the year ahead. Monks and nuns burn juniper and cedar as offerings, and perform sacred dances to overcome spiritual obstacles. In their homes, families and friends gather for a ceremony in which they throw *tsampa* (barley flour) is thrown into the air as they say aspirational prayers for the future, and make offerings of incense and butter lamps. The festivities go late into the night as people gather around large bonfires, singing, dancing, and drinking *chang,* a homemade brew, creating an atmosphere of celebration and renewal that continues for the next several days.

PRAYER FLAGS

Tibetan prayer flags are made from pieces of cotton and are imprinted by carved woodblocks with auspicious symbols and mantras that are meant to be carried by the wind. Prayer flags are said to bring long life, happiness, and prosperity to everyone in the surrounding area. Flags are hung from roofs, poles, and mountain tops. Yellow, green, red, white, and blue flags represent earth, water, fire, wind, and space respectively. Prayer flags known as *lung-ta*, meaning "windhorse," send the forces of compassion and wisdom to all beings. New flags replace the old ones during Losar, the Tibetan New Year.

Traditional Tibetan prayer flags *fly in the wind above the courtyard of a community center in Himachal Pradesh, India, during Losar, 1997. Tibetan men circle the central pole holding flags that had just been rigged, while throwing barley flour* (tsampa) *into the air.*

Prayer flags are sewn onto ropes *during Losar, the Tibetan New Year, in Himachal Pradesh, India, 1997.*

A cloud of smoke *rises from a pile of juniper, cedar, rhododendron, and other fragrant branches during preparations for the celebration of Losar.*

PASSING ON BUDDHISM TO CHILDREN

THE DALAI LAMA HAS EMPHASIZED the need for every Tibetan child to not only receive a modern education, but learn about their own cultural and spiritual heritage. One of the main reasons that Tibetan parents send their children into exile is so that they can grow up with the religious freedoms that they themselves are denied. It still remains to be seen, however, if this new generation, once given the choice, will embrace the Buddha's teachings. Many Tibetan orphans are being educated in monasteries in exile, but some worry that the children in secular schools are not learning to appreciate the deeper values of Buddhism.

THE CHALLENGE FOR EDUCATORS

"So many Tibetans have died. Now a new generation is growing up who do not know these things," said the late Taring Amala, who founded the Tibetan Homes Foundation. She speaks to the challenge of the Tibetan exiled community to pass on Buddhist values in ways that are relevant to their experience. "Tibetan children are saying

A child learns to prostrate while watching others at Tsuk Lhakhang, the main temple in Dharamsala, India, near the palace of His Holiness the Dalai Lama, 1997.

prayers like flags in the wind—they do not know the meaning." In pre-invasion Tibet, children began learning Buddhism through simple memorized recitation. Tibetan educators believe this needs to change. Taring Amala felt that "all the prayers that children learn must be explained to them. What they learn from memory does not help them." Jetsun Pema, the Dalai Lama's younger sister and director of the Tibetan Children's Village, agrees. "I think the way we teach Buddhism to children needs to evolve. If it doesn't evolve with the times, then it has no meaning. The essence shouldn't change, but the approach should change." Jetsun Pema cites some changes that have already been made. School prayer sessions are not as long as they were in the past. Once a week, the children recite prayers for about 40 minutes, for a special purpose—such as for the people who have died in Tibet, or for someone who is ill. Morning prayers have also been shortened, and more focus is placed on explaining the meaning behind them.

In Leh, Ladakh, India, Tibetan girls practice traditional dance at the Tibetan Children's Village School in 1997.

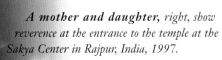

A mother and daughter, right, show reverence at the entrance to the temple at the Sakya Center in Rajpur, India, 1997.

PRESERVING BUDDHIST HEARTS & MINDS

The Dalai Lama has sent religious teachers to each school, and the approach to teaching Buddhism to children is becoming more open and nonsectarian, with classes receiving instruction from teachers on all Tibetan Buddhist traditions. Tibetan children are also beginning to learn basic meditation techniques. For Taring Amala, such initiatives did not come a moment too soon. "A lot of time has been wasted," she said. In this way, Jetsun Pema hopes that the children will become naturally drawn to the Dharma. "If you start forcing Buddhist instruction on children," she explains, "they won't practice from their own initiative and they won't achieve the depth of understanding." Whereas in traditional Tibetan society deeper spiritual understanding developed through years of practice and experience, there is a far greater danger in exile of children becoming disenchanted with their culture early on, and gravitating instead to worldly pastimes that appear to be initially more rewarding.

Taring Amala was not interested in turning her students into lamas, but in bringing fundamental spiritual values into their daily lives. "How do we teach our young people to be more compassionate, to be tolerant, to be helpful and honest? . . . Children have to know the basics of what Lord Buddha taught, such as the ten negative actions, which are similar to the Ten Commandments. Lord Buddha tells us that everything depends on our actions. If we do good, then the result will also be good. The children should be taught these things."

The Tibetan people were thrown into the modern age from a culture that was technologically far removed from the rest of the world, and that focused on inner rather than outer development. It is understandable that for Tibetan youth, the lure of Western-style culture and entertainment can be hypnotic. Educators are working to use modern communication media to provide children access to the legacy of Tibetan culture. "It's easy for our children to read comics or watch movies and get glued to the television, but how do you use these mediums to give them the right message?" says Jetsun Pema, echoing a universal parental concern. It is clear, however, that all Tibetan children share a deep love and reverence for the Dalai Lama. As Jetsun Pema notes with wry amusement, "We tell them something a hundred times, but His Holiness just has to tell them once and they get the message."

Children who attend the local Tibetan school in a refugee settlement, left, in Himachal Pradesh, India, wait to greet a representative from UNESCO, who visited the school that day, 1997.

*A **child learns** to write Tibetan script on a wooden tablet, India, 1991.*

TIBETAN ARTS & SCIENCES

བོད་ཀྱི་རྒྱུ་རྩལ་དང་མཚན་ཉིད།

T HE TIBETAN PEOPLE have surrounded themselves with imagery and symbolism intended to continually draw the mind towards its highest potential. Tibetan visual art, dance, language, festivals, and entertainment, as well as the arts of medicine and astrology, are saturated with Buddhist symbolism and meaning. Brilliantly colored paintings and intricate statues depict enlightened beings who gaze down from walls in homes and temples, while plays and dances reenact their life stories. Doctors treat patients while meditating on healing deities; in the Tibetan flag, snow lions guard the flame of enlightenment; and the language itself is imbued with a profound spiritual perspective. Even Tibetan currency was rich with Buddhist symbolism. For Tibetans, art is a means to an end—a tool on the path to finding complete freedom from suffering, and so it is considered meritorious to sponsor the making of holy objects. The artists themselves usually remain anonymous and pass down their skills quietly from generation to generation.

Every year, Tibetans perform dances in the courtyard outside the residence of His Holiness the Dalai Lama in Dharamsala, as an expression of reverence and as an offering to celebrate his birthday. These young women are performing in a 1997 celebration.

Dancers performing *for the birthday of His Holiness the Dalai Lama, Dharamsala, 1997. The dancers at left perform a dance from the Kirong region; the dancers above, from Utsang, 1997.*

TRADITIONAL DANCE

ALMOST EVERY TIBETAN KNOWS HOW TO DANCE. Tibetan dances are sometimes structured and formal, meant to be performed for special functions, and other times a dynamic and spontaneous expression of friends and family at intimate get-togethers. Traditionally, music and dance has not only provided entertainment, but also education in folklore and Tibetan history, a platform for political satire, and a way of carrying news from town to town. The 7th-century Tibetan king, Songtsen Gampo, reworked many traditional folk dances into a Buddhist framework, and although a number of dances have retained a religious significance, many relate to everyday secular events. The dance styles vary tremendously according to region, but the themes remain the same. Tibetans dance and sing songs during festivals such as Losar (Tibetan New Year), as well as during wedding celebrations. Some recurring themes of Tibetan dance are courtship rituals, as well as poignant observations of the natural world, its elements, and the animals that populate it. Some dances mark agricultural and seasonal phases, such as the autumn harvest when the villagers formed a circle and danced around the fields; Tibetan dances are often performed in a circle. On a happy occasion, such as the visit of a high lama, the Khampas of Eastern Tibet perform a large circle dance of up to 300 people for an entire day.

SONG

Tibetan village had a song leader who was acknowledged for exceptional vocal skill, and who would lead the chorus in songs and dances that sometimes lasted for many hours. Song contests are also a popular Tibetan event. Tibetan men and women stand in two lines facing one another and take turns singing a verse. Each side tries to outdo the other's performance in an often amusing exchange, creating a playful environment in which young men and women can meet one another.

A young Tibetan girl *performs a traditional dance from Kham, during the birthday celebration for His Holiness the Dalai Lama, 1997.*

Students from TIPA (*Tibetan Institute of Performing Arts*), *right, dance at Sherab Ling Monastery, in Himachal Pradesh, for the birthday of the 17th Karmapa, 1997.*

A dance groups performs a traditional dance from their homeland, Derge, Kham, in eastern Tibet, below. Himachal Pradesh, 1997.

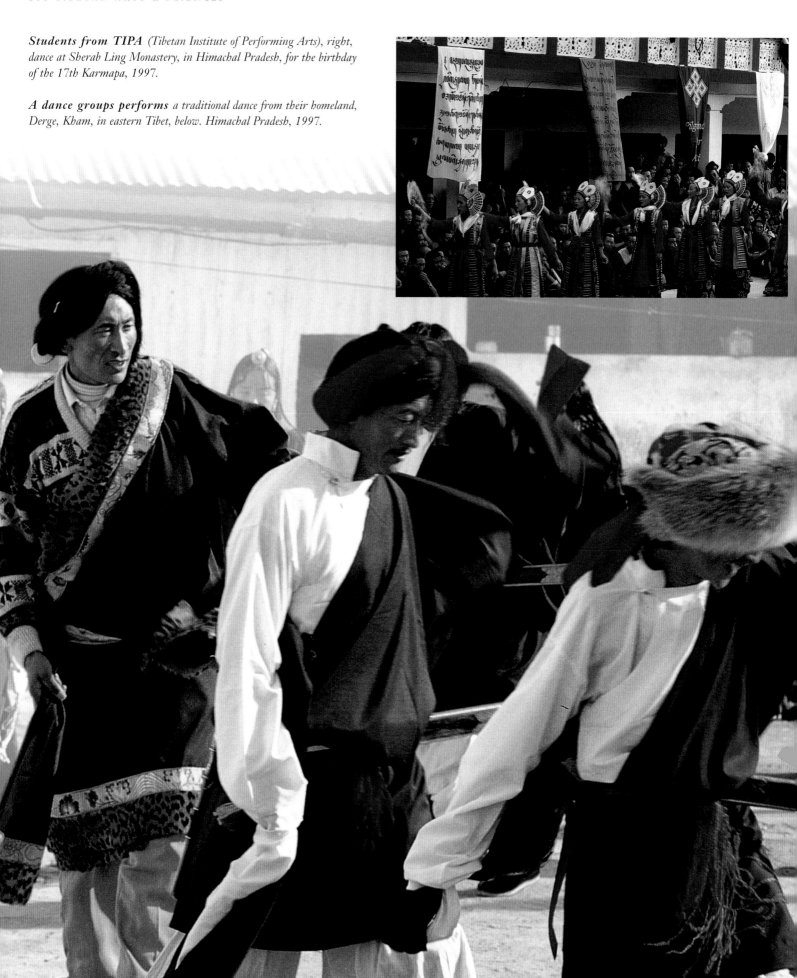

TIBETAN INSTITUTE OF PERFORMING ARTS

Performing arts are integral to the Tibetan cultural experience, from the awe-inspiring rituals of its monasteries to the vibrant celebrations of its local people. Since 1959, the Tibetan Institute of Performing Arts (TIPA) has worked to preserve the vivid and distinctive folk traditions of Tibet. The first institution established in exile, TIPA runs its own school of performing arts that offers classes and diplomas in Tibetan theater, dance, and music, alongside a modern classical education. The school is impressively self-sufficient, as students also learn how to make the masks and costumes as well as the musical instruments for the performances. In this way, the children gain an intimacy with all aspects of these cultural traditions. The institute has produced many talented performers, and a number of instructors trained at TIPA travel to settlements in India and Nepal to give workshops to refugee children. Classes for non-Tibetans have also recently been introduced. TIPA performs during Tibetan national holidays and festivals, and every April it holds the much-anticipated Folk Opera Festival in Dharamsala, when the whole town gathers to watch the colorful dances and plays. TIPA artists have given performances around the world and are beginning to receive international recognition.

The tradition of performing arts, *an important part of Tibetan Buddhist culture, is being preserved by the lay community, and TIPA plays a vital role in this effort. TIPA dancers, Sherab Ling Monastery, 1997.*

PERFORMING ARTS

I N THE WARMTH OF THE TIBETAN SUMMER, families would gather to watch dramatic performances of acting, dance, and song that mirror the human condition and bring to life the characters of Tibetan history and legend. This art form is commonly referred to as Tibetan opera, and its origins are lost in antiquity, although there is a legend about its beginnings. A 14th-century Tibetan scholar named Thangtong Gyelpo planned to build a bridge over every river in Tibet. However, after three years, he still could not raise the funds he needed for this endeavor. A female transcendental being appeared to him in a dream and told him about seven beautiful sisters who were expert dancers. Thangtong Gyelpo organized the sisters into a musical drama troupe to earn money for his bridges, which is why Tibetan opera is known as *lhamo,* meaning "goddess."

A CONTINUING TRADITION

In its early years, Tibetan opera mainly dealt with themes of simple local life, but over time it absorbed Buddhist narratives and evolved into a complex art form that offers a vibrant display of the Tibetan national character. The performers often act out the

A Tibetan musician accompanies opera dancers by playing a dranyen, *a type of Tibetan lute, Dharamsala, 1997.*

Two members of TIPA cloaked in full costume perform the classic snow lion dance, Dharamsala, 1997.

life stories of great Buddhist practitioners, called *namthar* or "lives of perfect liberation," but there are moments of satire and lightheartedness as well. Under the Sixth Dalai Lama, these troupes were encouraged, performing in courtyards of large monasteries or noble houses, as well as during *Zho-Ton,* the midsummer yogurt festival held in Lhasa. Traditionally, Tibetan opera was mostly vocal, the only musical accompaniment being a drum and cymbals. Today, performances may feature instruments such as lutes, fiddles, flutes, and even the occasional synthesizer or electric guitar. Nomadic bards traveled from village to village and sang, danced, and performed dynamic acrobatic displays. The most popular songs

A character from a Tibetan lhamo, or opera, captivates the crowd in Dharamsala, 1997. Lhamo is a favorite form of entertainment for Tibetans, and is also a way of keeping alive the stories which make up their cultural history.

include the spiritual poems of the famous hermit-yogi, Milarepa. There is also the classic Epic of King Gesar; called the national poem of Tibet, it recounts the exploits of a legendary Tibetan warrior. Tibetan oral traditions were preserved through familial lines until their songs began to be written down in the late 19th century. Though the bards themselves have all but disappeared, their stories have found a forum within operas and musical dramas. Whereas monastic music has remained untouched by time, secular music has found many new expressions, and in exile, modern jazz and rock as well as Indian music have all influenced traditional Tibetan styles.

These opera dancers are dressed in the costumes of the ngonpas, *Tibetan for "sons of heaven," representing hunters who traditionally dance at the beginning of an opera, Sherab Ling Monastery, 1997.*

ART IN MONASTERIES

THE SURVIVING TIBETAN BUDDHIST monasteries traditionally contain glorious murals of Buddhist iconography. A number of these are now centuries old. In the Himalayan regions outside Tibet, where Tibetan Buddhist culture has not been decimated, the effects of weather, aging, and simple wear and tear have, in many cases, taken an exacting toll. In Mustang, Nepal, a team of conservation experts have been working to restore wall paintings in a number of monasteries, being careful to match their techniques and materials with those traditionally used. The survival of these murals is intimately linked to the buildings themselves, some of which are in a serious state of disrepair. Before any work can begin on the murals, building repairs need to be made, with particular attention to the roofs. Only then can the effects of poor drainage, leaks, and rising damp be prevented from continuing to damage the monastery walls. These walls were made of rammed mud and mortar, and their thickness, which can be over three feet (91 cm) in places, greatly contributes to the overall strength of the building. The original artisans prepared the wall surfaces for painting by applying layers of plaster, using more or less the same method that the artists of Renaissance Europe employed. In fact, the murals of Tibetan Buddhism have been compared in quality to the works of the Renaissance Italian masters.

A shrine in a Ladakhi monastery is filled with holy statues, some of which are centuries old. Tibetan Buddhist statues were traditionally made of gilt copper or brass, and are often adorned with jewels, fine brocades, and khatas (scarves).

LADAKHI MONASTERIES

Ladakh is part of the arid Tibetan plateau and therefore is safe from the rains brought by monsoon. This dry environment has helped to preserve the monastic wall paintings; however, the walls do reveal some visible water damage and the murals are clearly in need of restoration. These monasteries also contain intricately carved wooden furniture and altars, and ancient scriptural texts stacked on shelves inset into the walls. In Ladakh, Buddhist art is a functional part of everyday monastic life. Here, you can see and feel what life must have been like in Tibet before the Chinese invasion.

This Ladakhi monastery is both a functioning monastic center and a treasury of priceless Tibetan Buddhist art. The shrine room, above, is embellished with richly colored patterns and Buddhist imagery. At the rear, statues are displayed in an ornate cabinet; an altar on the right is laden with flowers and khatas. Although the wall paintings are well-preserved, some water damage is evident.

A detail from the wall painting (seen at the center of the large picture) shows Avalokiteshvara with 11 heads, an image associated with the 11th-century Indian nun Lakshmi (Ani Palmo in Tibet), who developed a practice called Nyung-ne.

THANGKAS

THE KEY TO THE PRACTICE OF VAJRAYANA is visualization, and as such, artistic depictions of Buddhist deities and teachers are visual aids for the path to enlightenment. Images of Buddhist deities are not themselves objects of meditation, but templates for the deity that the practitioner creates in his or her mind—a three-dimensional animate being that can inspire spiritual understanding.

THANGKA AS TANTRIC ART

Tantric art is designed to be studied until the observer becomes intimately acquainted with its every detail. The complex visual imagery is to be utilized as a "manual" that the practitioner can read to become familiar with positive mental states at subtle levels of consciousness. Tibetan thangka-making is an ancient tantric art form of sacred images on cloth scrolls. Their subjects include holy beings, meditational deities, great teachers, and mandalas, and they traditionally adorned the walls of every monastery, nunnery, and household in Tibet. There are two types of thangkas: *gothang* (embroidered and appliquéd or woven with silk), and *trithang* (painted). The earliest thangkas were rolled and carried by nomadic Buddhists, so that they could continue to engage in practice during long trips.

Silk applique thangkas vary in size from from wall-sized to giant thangkas measuring as long as 154 x 180 feet (47 x 55 m), such as the giant thangka, above, pictured in this early photograph from Tibet. Painted thangkas can be smaller than one foot (30 cm) in height and are typically no larger than 7 x 10 feet (2 x 3 m).

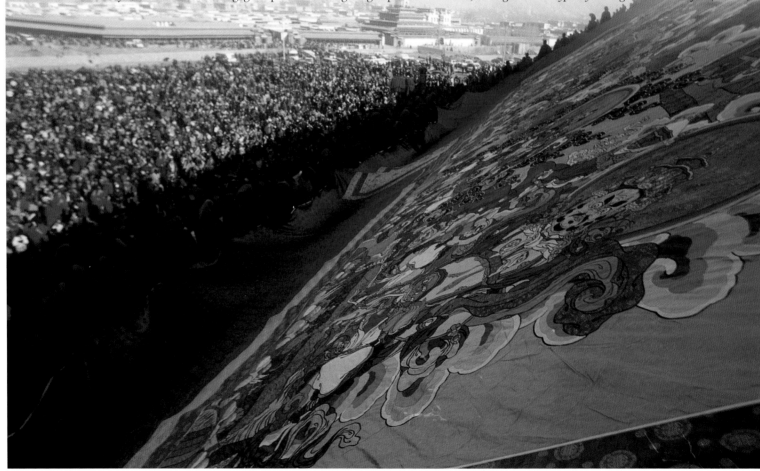

Most Tibetan monasteries owned a variety of thangkas for ceremonies and public worship. Large thangkas were displayed on monastery walls, while giant thangkas were unfurled on hillsides. Many were destroyed during and after the invasion, although this tradition is now being revived; old thangkas are being restored and new ones created, such as the one above, Tibet, 2002. At right, monks at the Sherab Ling Monastery in India raise a large thangka during a ceremony, 1997.

ORIGINS OF THANGKA ART

It is said that the first painted images of the Buddha were created in India during his lifetime. Buddhist artistic iconography is believed to have reached Tibet in the 7th century, during the reign of King Songtsen Gampo. The King's Nepali and Chinese Buddhist wives ushered in a wave of artists from their countries, and Tibet experienced a renaissance of sacred art. The tradition was threatened in the early 9th century by King Lang Darma, who usurped the throne, abolished Buddhist practice, and destroyed most Buddhist art. This dark age lasted almost 200 years. A second Buddhist renaissance took place in the 11th century. Under the reign of Tibetan king Yeshe O, the great translator, Rinchen Zangpo, travelled to Kashmir and returned with dozens of artists. He built new monasteries, and Buddhist art began to flourish. For the next 700 years, six major schools of thangka painting were developed by the influential Tibetan artists of the day. Tibetan thangka painters originally followed early Indian artistic styles, with subsequent influence from Chinese and Nepalese artists; eventually a unique Tibetan style developed, deeply informed by Tibetan Buddhist culture.

***Thangkas are framed** in elaborate silk brocades; sometimes they are covered with silk veils. This contemporary thangka of Shakyamuni Buddha hangs above statues of Tsongkhapa (center) with his two chief disciples.*

CREATION OF A THANGKA PAINTING

Each thangka is based on a prescribed pattern, with specified colors, forms, compositions, gestures, and symbols; the method of creating thangkas is also defined in detail. The first step is to prepare the canvas; the cloth is washed, stretched, and sewn onto a wooden frame, then primed and polished with a smooth stone. Before a thangka is painted, a precise geometrical grid is drawn on the cloth in charcoal or pencil. This grid, considered sacred in itself, acts as the blueprint for the deity or mandala to be painted within its boundaries, and provides a template for the scale and proportions needed to attain the required symmetry and balance. Novice thangka artists may

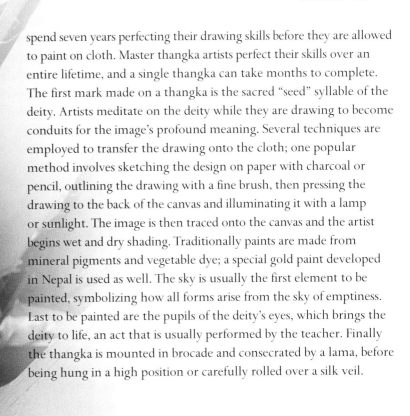

spend seven years perfecting their drawing skills before they are allowed to paint on cloth. Master thangka artists perfect their skills over an entire lifetime, and a single thangka can take months to complete. The first mark made on a thangka is the sacred "seed" syllable of the deity. Artists meditate on the deity while they are drawing to become conduits for the image's profound meaning. Several techniques are employed to transfer the drawing onto the cloth; one popular method involves sketching the design on paper with charcoal or pencil, outlining the drawing with a fine brush, then pressing the drawing to the back of the canvas and illuminating it with a lamp or sunlight. The image is then traced onto the canvas and the artist begins wet and dry shading. Traditionally paints are made from mineral pigments and vegetable dye; a special gold paint developed in Nepal is used as well. The sky is usually the first element to be painted, symbolizing how all forms arise from the sky of emptiness. Last to be painted are the pupils of the deity's eyes, which brings the deity to life, an act that is usually performed by the teacher. Finally the thangka is mounted in brocade and consecrated by a lama, before being hung in a high position or carefully rolled over a silk veil.

Before the Cultural Revolution, thangka painters were members of prestigious art guilds. All traditional art practice was banned in Tibet by the Chinese until the 1970s. At the Norbulingka Institute near Dharamsala, in India, left, thangka painting students paint up to eleven hours a day using raw materials obtained from Tibet.

This ancient thangka, like all Tibetan Buddhist artwork, is unsigned, as Buddhist art is not a tool for self-expression, but a visual aid for the path to enlightenment.

A cast gilt copper Bodhisattva from Tibet, seated on a lotus in the "royal ease" pose, c. 14th–15th century.

SCULPTURE

TIBETAN BUDDHIST SCULPTURES, like thangkas, are visual guideposts that assist the practitioner in the quest for enlightenment. In addition, the commissioning of a Buddhist artwork for a temple is thought to bring the patron merit; the donation of a metalwork brings even greater merit. The production of metal in Tibet dates back to around the 1st century BC. Tibetan metalsmiths worked in gold, silver, iron, and copper, and were known for their fine armor, weapons, and jewelry. The first Buddhist sculptures most likely came to Tibet in the 7th century as part of the dowry of King Songtsen Gampo's Chinese bride, including the most precious sculpture in Tibet, a gilt statue of Shakyamuni Buddha (see page 135).

SCULPTURAL TRADITION IN TIBET

During the 11th century, many Nepali and Indian sculptors came to Tibet to work on the new monasteries and temples being erected during the second Buddhist renaissance, and Tibetan artisans were trained in sculpting religious metal statuary and temple implements. By the 14th century, Tibetan sculptors had mastered this art, which reached a zenith during the building of the Potala Palace in the 17th century. Intricate wood carving was also a refined art in the construction of sacred architecture.

The tradition of apprenticeship in metalcraft is sustained by Tibetans in exile; apprentices study for up to 2 years with master craftsmen before graduating to the master level. When a large statue is completed, it is filled with mantras, prayers, and other holy relics. Groups of laypeople and monks may work for months to fill a large statue. They print thousands of mantras and prayers, cut them into narrow strips, and roll them into tight rolls wrapped with cloth. Like stupas, a large statue

A Tibetan artisan painting a wooden phurpa, a sacred ritual instrument used in tantric ceremonies to spiritually vanquish enemies.

A detail of sculptural relief on the brass bell tower on the roof of the Jokhang, in Lhasa, left. The animals in the center are from the Jataka Tales, which recount the previous lives of the Buddha.

Offerings left by pilgrims adorn a large gilt statue of Padmasambhava, below, at Tso Pema, India, in a cave where he is believed to have been on retreat.

has a central wooden axis pole—a "tree of life"—that is also covered in mantras and wrapped in silk. Special mantras are attached to the inside of the statue's eyes and ears, and the rest of the space is filled with precious stones, herbs, flowers, and other objects. During the consecration ritual, a lama meditates on the deity and requests it to enter the statue. The face of the statue is then unveiled and the lama will make the finishing touches on the pupils, symbolizing the opening of the eyes of enlightened wisdom.

TSA TSAS

Another type of sculpture ubiquitous among Tibet Buddhists are small votive painted-clay tablets called *tsa tsas,* which are also popular among Burmese and Thai Buddhists. This art form probably originated in India, and the earliest examples date back to the 8th century. As with all Tibetan Buddhist art, the creation of tsa tsas is believed to generate great positive energy for the creator and the environment. Miniature images of Buddhas and deities are made with a precisely proportioned metal mold so that the image can be perfectly reproduced every time. They are placed inside statues and stupas, around pilgrimage sites, in sacred caves, on altars, and are sometimes attached frieze-style to monastery walls. Small tsa tsas may be inserted into a portable shrine called a *gow* that Buddhists bring with them on journeys, or carried as a type of protective amulet. Tsa tsas that are made by great teachers or that contain their ashes are considered particularly sacred, and these are often distributed among the students as objects of meditation. Tsa tsas are consecrated by inserting a roll of prayers or mantras into a hole at the base if the tsa tsa is large enough, or by painting a mantra on the tsa tsa's flat reverse side.

RITUAL ART

TORMA & BUTTER SCULPTURE

TORMAS ARE INTRICATELY HAND-MOLDED ornaments used as offerings in religious ceremonies. Traditionally made from barley-flour *(tsampa)* and butter, altar tormas are generally no more than six inches (15 cm) high, and there are different tormas for different deities, each with its own special symbolism. The three main elements of the torma, however—its base, its body, and its decoration—always represent enlightened qualities of body, speech, and mind. The purpose of offering tormas to enlightened beings is to develop generosity and receive spiritual inspiration. Tormas are also used as purification devices, and during ritual practice, practitioners visualize transferring their negative actions into these objects. On the 29th day of the last month of the year, many monasteries and temples perform a "casting away torma" to purify the negativities of the past year.

BUTTER SCULPTURE

Butter sculptures are a special kind of torma made by Tibetan monastics on auspicious occasions. Molded from dyed butter and tsampa, these sculptures can stand as high as 30 feet (9 m), the transient nature of their main ingredient a reminder of the impermanence of all phenomena. Many monasteries produce these tormas for the annual Butter Sculpture Festival, part of New Year celebrations. This was traditionally held in Kumbum in Eastern Tibet on the 15th day of the first month of the Tibetan calendar, so it is known as "The Offering of the Fifteenth." The festival is held at the town's main monastery on the site where the great 14th-century Tibetan Buddhist master, Tsongkhapa, is believed to have been born. A number of monastic colleges compete with each other to make the most ornate and beautiful sculptures.

A monk at Sherab Ling Monastery, Himachal Pradesh, puts the finishing touches to a large butter sculpture, 1997. Wearing masks is an act of reverence and prevents the artists from breathing on the images.

A monk lights incense on an altar during the Nyingma Monlam for World Peace, at Bodghaya, India, 1997. The altar is arrayed with butter sculptures decorated with intricately wrought disks and crowns of floral design. In between the larger butter sculptures are smaller gray tormas with white disks in groups of threes. All of the sculptures will be melted down at the end of the ceremony as a demonstration of the ephemeral nature of being.

The images are carefully hand-sculpted from hardened butter and then colored with natural dyes mixed with ash. The dyes for the more important figures are sometimes mixed with powdered gold or silver and other precious substances. Each year the displays center around a different theme, such as the previous life stories and great deeds of Shakyamuni Buddha, Tibetan Buddhist folk tales, and historical religious events. The sculptures can also be humorous and they often also include comic images of monastic life, with caricatures of head lamas and mobile figures that the monks can move by way of ropes, springs, and pulleys. The sculptures are only displayed for a few hours at night and are melted down before dawn the following day—a visual reminder of the impermanence of all things. At the end of the festival, a pyramidal stick structure called a *zor* is thrown into a pit and then burned. Inside the zor is a torma, which is made to absorb the previous year's negativities through a ritual ceremony. The fire represents the light of wisdom, which can eliminate and purify negative forces.

Monks make tormas at the Palyul Chokor Ling Nyingmapa Monastery in Himachal Pradesh, 1997. Tormas, molded ornaments that are offered to deities and used in purification ceremonies, are sculpted from dough made from tsampa and butter.

MANTRAS IN STONE & ARCHITECTURE

THE MAKING OF *MANI* STONES is a unique folk art that is intimately linked to Tibetan spiritual life. They are called mani stones because they are usually inscribed with Tibetan letters spelling OM MANI PADME HUM, the mantra of Avalokiteshvara, the Buddha of Compassion. They can also include other Tibetan Buddhist script and images. Mani stones consist of engravings or shallow reliefs on single large boulders, rock faces, or smaller stones, which are then painted. Mani-stone artisans have passed down their skills through generations. Altars of mani stones are often found near natural features such as hilltops, mountain passes, lakesides, and rivers banks, and are very common in remote regions of Eastern Tibet, where the local people built them as a focus for spiritual practice.

A woman expresses her complete devotion to Padmasambhava as she prostrates herself before a mani stone bearing his image at Tso Pema, where he is believed to have manifested from a lotus. Himachal Pradesh, India, 1997.

MANTRAS ON SACRED BUILDINGS

Mantras are also often carved around the roofs of Tibetan monasteries. These days, due to the scarcity of wood in India and the deforestation of Tibet, concrete is replacing traditional materials, threatening the survival of Tibet's rich wood-carving tradition. In the late 1980s, a number of young craftsman began arriving in India from Tibet to study traditional crafts, hoping to one day return to assist in the reconstruction of monasteries and temples that were damaged or destroyed during the Chinese decimation of Tibetan culture.

A Tibetan artisan uses a hammer and chisel, left, to form a relief of sacred Buddhist text in stone.

A monk paints a monastery exterior, right. In Tibet, temple structures were usually carved of wood; in India, Tibetans adapted by sculpting and carving cement.

SACRED TEXTS

A CCORDING TO A TIBETAN LEGEND, sometime between the 2nd and 3rd century, a Buddhist text fell from the sky onto the palace roof of a Tibetan king, Totori Nyentsen. However, because the text was in Sanskrit, no one could understand it. Four hundred years later, the first Tibetan written language came into being through the dedicated efforts of the 7th-century Buddhist king, Songtsen Gampo, who realized that the multitude of spoken dialects in Tibet made it almost impossible to effectively propagate the Dharma. He recognized that Tibet needed its own common language, and sent his minister, Thonmi Sambhota, to India to develop a Tibetan alphabet. Thonmi Sambhota came up with a system of 30 consonant glyphs and four vowels with methods to combine the two in 256 ways. Dots or dashes denoted the beginning of a new syllable. The script read left to right in elegant strokes that could be made thick or thin by the turning a brush or the nib of a bamboo pen. In some cases, the inks were made from precious stones such as turquoise, gold, and silver, to denote the preciousness of the Dharma that was being expressed.

Tibetan religious texts are traditionally printed in ink from carved wood blocks on both sides of separate rectangular sheets. *Called* pechas, *the narrow shape of the paper—traditionally made from root fiber—was modeled after early Indian sacred texts, which were printed on long palm leaves and introduced to Tibet in the 7th century.*

A RENAISSANCE OF TIBETAN LANGUAGE

The grammatical system that Thonmi Sambhota created caught on rapidly in Tibet and was soon being widely used, eventually spreading into other Himalayan kingdoms, marking the beginning of a thousand years of translation activity in Tibet. Tibetan calligraphers began to create many different styles of scripts for different purposes. There was a special script for sacred texts, for example, one for official decrees, and another for correspondence. Songtsen Gampo's work was continued by the 9th-century Tibetan king, Relbachen, who created a Sanskrit and Tibetan glossary of terms and revised the grammar and syntax of the written language to more closely resemble Sanskrit. Over the ensuing centuries, there was a lively and industrious exchange between India and Tibet, with translation teams made up of Indian and Tibetan scholars. For the most part, the Indians focused on making sure

A monk brushes water mixed with special medicinal herbs onto scriptures to sanctify them and, after they dry, rolls the sheets and places them inside a statue, northern India, 1997.

that the translations were doctrinally accurate, while the Tibetans maintained grammatical correctness. Between the 11th and 13th centuries, many scriptural texts were brought from India to Tibet to safeguard them against the invading Islamic armies. These texts were translated into Tibetan and preserved in Tibetan monasteries. After 1959, India returned the favor and became a haven for sacred Tibetan texts that were being destroyed in their homeland. In the 14th century, the Tibetan Buddhist scholar, Buton Rinchen Drup, compiled the scriptural translations into two divisions: the Kangyur and the Tengyur, which make up the Tibetan Buddhist canon. The Kangyur is the translated words of the Buddha, and the Tengyur contains translations of Indian Buddhist texts and commentaries. The creation of a Tibetan written language was a landmark in the development of Buddhism in Tibet. It allowed for Buddhist literature to be made available to ordinary people, not just Sanskrit scholars, much in the same way that translations of the Bible from Latin made it possible for the laity to study Christian scripture.

A Tibetan monk in Himachal Pradesh, India, recites scripture while he turns a prayer wheel, 1997.

Wrapped texts at the 17th-century Pemayangtse Monastery library in Sikkim, India. After the Chinese invasion, Tibet's invaluable literary heritage was at risk of being destroyed, as libraries were largely scattered. Massive efforts by both Tibetans and non-Tibetans in the private and public sectors have succeeded in rescuing tens of thousands of books, many of which were redistributed to monasteries in exile. Additional preservation efforts have resulted in the reprinting or scanning of texts.

ASTROLOGICAL SCIENCE

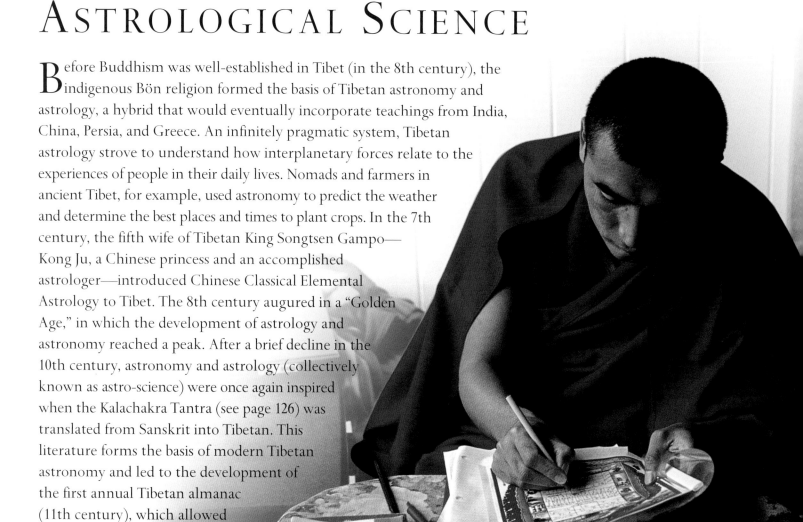

Before Buddhism was well-established in Tibet (in the 8th century), the indigenous Bön religion formed the basis of Tibetan astronomy and astrology, a hybrid that would eventually incorporate teachings from India, China, Persia, and Greece. An infinitely pragmatic system, Tibetan astrology strove to understand how interplanetary forces relate to the experiences of people in their daily lives. Nomads and farmers in ancient Tibet, for example, used astronomy to predict the weather and determine the best places and times to plant crops. In the 7th century, the fifth wife of Tibetan King Songtsen Gampo—Kong Ju, a Chinese princess and an accomplished astrologer—introduced Chinese Classical Elemental Astrology to Tibet. The 8th century augured in a "Golden Age," in which the development of astrology and astronomy reached a peak. After a brief decline in the 10th century, astronomy and astrology (collectively known as astro-science) were once again inspired when the Kalachakra Tantra (see page 126) was translated from Sanskrit into Tibetan. This literature forms the basis of modern Tibetan astronomy and led to the development of the first annual Tibetan almanac (11th century), which allowed

*A **Tibetan monk** begins the complex task of calculating an astrological chart. Today this skill is revered by the Tibetan community as much as it was thousands of years ago.*

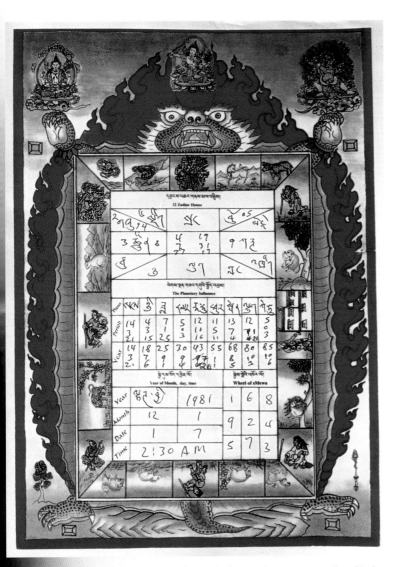

This Tibetan astrological chart *takes into account the subject's birth date and the precise location of the planets at the time of birth (among many other factors), to give a detailed picture of how life might unfold within the larger context of the calendar.*

astrologers to determine the exact positions of celestial bodies. So, although Tibetans name their years according to the Chinese astrological system, they follow the cycles of the Indian calendar. In the 17th century, the Fifth Dalai Lama's regent compiled a folio of Tibetan astrology, which is still in use today.

EVERYDAY USES OF ASTROLOGY

In Tibet, the local astrologer is usually a lama who is responsible for drawing up the ceremonial monastic calendar. In everyday life, astrologers are consulted for horoscopes of newborn babies, to advise about marriages and deaths, and to calculate auspicious dates for any number of important individual and community events, whether it is planting a crop, taking a trip, or starting a new business. Using information about an individual's time and place of birth, an astrologer can make predictions in four general areas: life energy, health, finances, and success. If he finds an imbalance in any of these, he will recommend an antidote that might entail, among other spiritual practices, performing a ritual such as a *puja* (giving an offering) or engaging in an act of generosity. When there is a death, Tibetans consult an astrologer in order to determine the correct ceremonial approach to burial or cremation. All medical students study astrology, and like Tibetan doctors, astrologers use the interaction of the five elements (wood, fire, earth, metal, and water) in their calculations, not only to offer spiritual and ceremonial guidance, but to provide practical methods of reducing suffering. Tibetan astrology is practiced from Mongolia to Zanskar.

TIBETAN MEDICINE

T IBETAN MEDICINE originated with the indigenous culture, Bön, as far back as 300 BC, although later contributions from traditional Chinese and, especially, Indian (Ayurvedic) medicine exerted an even more powerful influence on shaping the Tibetan model. Ayurvedic principles established the basis for analyzing physical disorders and suggesting treatments, while Buddhism, especially after it was established as the state religion by King Trisong Detsen in 792, greatly affected the concept of spirituality as a component of wellness. Tibetan medicine promotes the idea that ill health is far more than a physical condition, and diseases are regarded as symptoms rather than fixed entities. Tibetan doctors treat mental health and physical health as integral to one another: The body is not viewed as a compilation of separate parts, but as an interdependent and dynamic system of energies that are in continual communication with one another. For a Tibetan doctor, diseases represent imbalances of subtle psychological, physical, and environmental forces that ultimately depend upon the patient's

This early Tibetan thangka of the Medicine Buddha hangs in the Tibetan Medical Institute in Dharamsala, India. Tibetan Buddhists pray to the medicine Buddha for healing.

A monk holds a Tibetan medicine book (from the Dolpo region of Nepal) showing a plant and a musk deer. Not all ingredients in Tibetan medicine are herbal: musk from this particular deer is used for its aromatic properties; the meat is considered a tonic food.

DR. TENZIN CHODAK

For Dr. Tenzin Chodak, years of exile and hardship ended in 1982 with the resumption of his duties as the personal physician to His Holiness the Dalai Lama, a role that had come to an abrupt end in 1959, after the brutal suppression of the Tibetan nationalist movement by the Chinese government. As a result of this upheaval, Dr. Chodak, a gifted physician, who had been trained at the Lhasa Medical Institute, was confined for 21 years in Chinese prisons and labor camps until the late 1970s, when conditions grew marginally better, especially after the death of Mao Zedong, the Chairman of the Chinese Communist Party, in 1976. Released in 1980, Dr. Chodak returned to training students in the tradition of Tibetan medicine, especially the arts in which he has always excelled— pulse reading and medicinal formulation.

H.H. the Dalai Lama's personal physician

The hospital pharmacy at Mendzekhang, Lhasa, dispenses traditional Tibetan medicine—a vast pharmacopoeia that includes decoctions, powders, and pills. All Tibetan physicians have a wide knowledge of medicinal herbs and plants. Some remedies also incorporate precious stones and minerals.

state of mind for a cure. Tibetan medicine is receiving increasingly more international attention due to is efficacy in treating diseases that do not generally respond well to Western medicine.

DIAGNOSIS & TREATMENT

Dietary, behavioral, social, psychological, and environmental factors are all taken into account when making a diagnosis. In keeping with this holistic outlook, Tibetan medical drugs are made from aggregates of the same cosmic energies that constitute all phenomena: earth, air, fire, water, and space. These drugs, which are composed of ingredients such as soil, herbs, precious metals, sap, and bark, are used to combat the symptoms of unbalanced "humors"— wind, bile, and phlegm—as they manifest within the body. Disorders are the result of an excess of one humor or perhaps all three, while good health can be achieved through a balance of the humors. In order to diagnose a disease, doctors are trained to observe which humors are out of balance by examining a patient's complexion, tongue, eyes, ears, nails, and urine. Then, using a very subtle method of reading the pulse, Tibetan doctors are able to glean a wealth of information about each of the body's organs. Treatments range from diet and lifestyle modifications to the prescription of medicines, spiritual practice, massage, and moxibustion, the application of heat to certain points on the body.

Men sort traditional drugs at the Tibetan Medical and Astrological Institute, in Dharamsala, India, c. 1989. About two-thirds of the raw materials used in Tibetan formulas are imported from India and China.

TIBETAN BUDDHISM IN THE WORLD

ཨེ་མ་སྐྱིད་དུ་དར་བ་ལྷོ་བོད་བཅུད་ཟར་བསྲུ་ན།

T HE TIBETAN DIASPORA not only brought Tibetans into exile, but it has resulted in the spread of Tibetan Buddhism around the world. While it is a tragedy for the people of Tibet, it is an incredible blessing for people everywhere that this precious body of spiritual traditions is being shared so broadly. A number of great Tibetan masters who went into exile have been inspired by the depth of commitment of many non-Tibetan students of the Dharma, some of whom have become accomplished Dharma teachers in their own right. The masters recognize that a sincere practitioner is no less important to the continuation of the tradition just because they are not Tibetan. Tibetans who have settled in Europe (especially in Switzerland), North America, and Australia, are finding the opportunities to improve the material quality of their lives after a difficult existence as refugees in India. Many people who come to know Tibetans feel inspired to help them in their struggle to preserve their culture and advance their cause for human rights in Tibet. Tibetan Buddhism as a way of life is endangered and needs the support of the world community for its very survival.

The late Kalu Rinpoche (center) with Tibetan and Western disciples performing a ceremony to consecrate a stupa in Santa Fe, New Mexico, 1986.

Presenting His Holiness with khatas upon his arrival at JFK Airport in 1999 are, from left to right: Tenzing Chhodak, Director of The Tibet Fund, New York; Rinchen Dharlo, President of the Tibet Fund; Khyongla Rato Rinpoche, founder of the Tibet Center, New York; and Richard Gere, founder of the Gere Foundation, New York. His Holiness came to New York to give teachings at the Beacon Theater and a public talk in Central Park.

THE PRESERVATION OF TIBETAN BUDDHISM

In less than half a century, Tibetan Buddhism in the world has developed into a serious movement with a dynamic network of centers, teachers, and students. At the same time, however, it is being transmitted by the last of the great Tibetan Buddhist masters who were trained in Tibet before the Chinese invasion. We are at a precious moment in time when these few masters are still with us; within a short number of years they will be gone. It is critical to document these masters who are repositories of Tibetan Buddhist traditions, and preserve their teachings for future generations. Tibetans and non-Tibetans alike are helping in this effort, translating scripture and building archives of surviving sacred texts and art. One of the great challenges of Tibetans in exile is to maintain their spiritual life and values while cut off from the cultural support offered by their traditional communities. At the same time, exiled Tibetans are making important cultural contributions internationally. There is a growing interest in Tibetan Buddhism among the Chinese people inside and outside China, and this development is welcomed by Tibetans who hope that it will foster a new openness from China's leaders. Books and films about Tibet and Tibetan Buddhism are being published and distributed around the world. *The Art of Happiness* by His Holiness the Dalai Lama, for example, was one of the best-selling self-help books in publishing history. This "simple Buddhist monk" is having an extraordinary impact on the world and attracts enormous crowds wherever he goes. His Holiness is not interested in converting people to Buddhism, however. Rather he recommends that unless they have a strong personal calling to Buddhism, people should keep their own spiritual traditions, and work to create a universal common ground through developing "a good heart." His message of compassion and universal responsibility is striking a chord with people everywhere. The Tibetan cause has been adopted by many Hollywood celebrities, but thousands of ordinary people are finding themselves genuinely transformed by their exposure to this deeply spiritual culture—one which offers a measure of sanity and goodness in a world fraught with fear and uncertainty.

At a rally for freedom in Tibet, a Tibetan girl holds a photograph of the six-year-old boy recognized as the reincarnation of the Panchen Lama, Tibet's second highest-ranking spiritual leader. In 1995, the boy was arrested by Chinese authorities and another candidate was chosen to replace him. An international campaign is trying to secure his freedom. Palden Gyatso, left, spent 33 years in Chinese prisons. Santa Monica, 1997.

In 1993, His Holiness attended a meeting of the Parliament of World's Religions in Chicago. During his trip he gave a talk in an outdoor park. Among the crowd who came to hear him was this Tibetan woman who lives in Chicago.

Lama Gyatso, with Western students, release fish meant to be used as bait back into the ocean as an expression of compassion— the rescuing of endangered animals is a common Buddhist practice.

GLOSSARY

Axis Mundi: central hub of the universe.

Atisha: 11th-century Indian scholar who brought about the second wave of Buddhism in Tibet.

Avalokiteshvara: the Buddha of compassion; the patron deity of Tibet.

bardo: transitional state between death and rebirth (sometimes also the periods between significant life phases).

Bodhgaya: the site of the Buddha's enlightenment in India.

Bön: the indigenous spiritual tradition of Tibet, which shares many teachings with Buddhism.

Bönpo: a practitioner of Bön.

butter sculpture: a type of *torma* made from butter and barley flour, for use on auspicious occasions.

Chod: a practice aimed at overcoming attachment to the physical body and thus to the sense of an independent self.

Chorten: Tibetan for stupa, a Buddhist monument often containing the relics of high lamas.

chupas: traditional Tibetan dress.

Dalai Lama: the highest ranking spiritual and political authority of Tibet, and head of all schools of Tibetan Buddhism.

datsans: a Mongolian term for Buddhist monasteries.

Dharma: has various definitions, but commonly refers to the Buddha's teachings.

Dharmakaya: truth body, or ultimate nature of all phenomena.

Drogmi: 11th-century translator who brought Lamdre teachings to Tibet.

Dzogchen: the highest and most advanced practice in the Nyingma system.

gelong: a fully ordained monk.

Gelug: Tibetan Buddhist school founded by Tsongkhapa in the 14th century.

geshe: the highest degree in the Gelug monastic system.

getsul: a novice monk.

gothang: a type of thangka in which the sacred image is embroidered and appliquéd or woven in silk.

gow: a portable shrine.

Guru Rinpoche: an epithet of Padmasambhava meaning "Precious Teacher."

Hinayana: with Mahayana, one of the two divisions of Buddhism. Hinayana teachings emphasize personal liberation from suffering; *see* Theravada.

Jowo Mikyoe Dorjee: highly revered statue of Buddha as eight-year-old child, contained in the Johkang in Lhasa, Tibet.

Kadam: a now-extinct school of Tibetan Buddhism, founded in the 11th century by Atisha.

Kagyu: a school of Tibetan Buddhism founded by Marpa the Translator in the 10th century.

Kalachakra: lit.: "cycles of time," a meditational deity and advanced tantric practice associated with world peace.

Kalu Rinpoche: a great 20th century master of the Kagyu school.

Karma Kagyu: one of the four subschools of the Dagpo Kagyu lineage presided over by the Karmapa.

Karmapa: the head of the Karma Kagyu lineage of the Kagyu school, whom many Tibetans revere as a living Buddha.

khata: a white silk scarf used as an offering on special occasions.

khenpo: the title given to a highly learned scholar of Tibetan Buddhism in the Nyingma, Kagyu, and Sakya schools. In the Gelug school, can refer to an abbot.

Konchok Gyalpo: constructed the first Sakya Monastery and considered the founder of the Sakya tradition.

Lamdre: lit.: "path and fruit," a Sakya practice emphasizing the interconnectedness of enlightened and unenlightened existence.

Lamrim: lit.: "stages of the path," a system of teachings used in the Gelug school, outlining the path to enlightenment in a series of steps.

Lang Darma: a 10th-century Tibetan king who tried to wipe out Tibetan Buddhism in Tibet

lhamo: Tibetan opera.

Lharam Geshe: the highest *geshe* level in the Gelug school.

Losar: Tibetan New Year.

Madhyamaka: a school of Indian Buddhism founded by Nagarjuna in 2nd century, which strongly influenced Tibetan Buddhism and presents a "Middle Way" between nonexistence (nihilism) and independent existence (absolutism).

Mahamudra: lit.: "great seal." A system of profound meditational practice popular in the Kagyu and Gelug schools.

Mahayana: with Hinayana, one of the two divisions of Buddhism, emphasizing the attainment of complete enlightenment to save all sentient beings from suffering.

Mandala: lit.: "circle." Meditational deities and their abode, sometimes represented in colored sand, symbolizing the enlightened mind and pure perception and used to aid meditation.

mani: short for the mantra of Avalokiteshvara, *Om Mani Padme Hum.*

mani stone: a stone engraved and painted usually with *Om Mani Padme Hum.*

Middle Way: *see* Madhyamaka.

Milarepa: 12th-century yogi-saint whose spiritual songs are beloved in all schools of Tibetan Buddhism.

Monlam: an important prayer festival held after Losar, established by Tsongkhapa.

Mount Kailash: Tibet's most sacred mountain and a popular pilgrimage site.

Nagarjuna: 2nd-century Indian master credited with the establishment of the Madhyamaka school.

namthar: biographic stories of great Tibetan Buddhist practitioners often depicted in Tibetan opera.

Nechung Oracle: the State Oracle, an important medium and advisor to the Dalai Lama, who channels the spirit of Dorje Drakden, a protector deity of Tibet and the Dharma.

nirvana: state of permanent liberation from suffering and its causes (the afflicted mind).

Ngakpas: masters of Dzogchen who as lay practitioners and householders may marry and have children, but must spend a great deal of time in retreat.

Nyingma: oldest of the four Tibetan Buddhist schools, established in the 8th century and based on the teachings of Padmasambhava.

Nyingmapa: practitioner of Nyingma.

Olmo Lung Ring: mythical home of Tonpa Shenrab Miwo, founder of Bön.

Padmasambhava: 8th-century Indian master, who first brought Buddhism to Tibet.

Panchen Lama: second highest-ranking Tibetan Buddhist spiritual figure after the Dalai Lama.

puja: ritual prayer offering.

Rime: a nonsectarian movement started in 19th century, favoring the integration of all four schools of Tibetan Buddhism.

Rinchen Zangpo: a great 11th-century Tibetan translator.

Sakya: one of the four schools of Tibetan Buddhism, established in the 11th century.

Sakya Pandita: a 13th century-Sakya master who became the spiritual guide to the grandson of Genghis Khan.

samsara: the repetitive cycle of suffering to which we are bound through unenlightened existence.

sangha: the community of monks and nuns; also refers to those who have realized the ultimate nature of reality.

Sarnath: a place in Northern India, near present-day Varanasi, where Buddha gave his first teaching

Shakyamuni Buddha: the historical Buddha, also known as Siddhartha, who reached enlightenment over 2,500 years ago.

Shambhala: a mythical utopian land linked to the teachings of Kalachakra.

Shantarakshita: an 8th-century Indian abbot who helped to establish Buddhism in Tibet.

Shantideva: an 8th-century Indian Buddhist master, author of *A Guide to the Bodhisattva's Way of Life*.

Shenlha Okar: Bön deity of compassion.

Sonam Gyatso: the second reincarnation of one of Tsongkhapa's main disciples and the 3rd Dalai Lama.

Songtsen Gampo: a 7th-century Tibetan king who converted to Buddhism.

Stupa: *see chorten.*

tantra: *see Vajrayana.*

terma: a text or sacred object left by Padmasambhava and his consort, Yeshe Tsolgyal, for future generations of practitioners to discover.

terton: "treasure finder," one who discovers a terma in the physical realm or through spiritual revelation.

thangka: a silk or painted cloth scroll, often mounted in brocade, bearing sacred Tibetan Buddhist images. They are devotional objects; the symbols and gestures depicted are meant to represent manifestations of Buddhist principles.

Theravada: the only remaining school of Hinayana.

Thonmi Sambhota: 7th-century Tibetan minister, developed Tibetan alphabet.

togden: member of a yogi lineage, who practices a particularly spartan form of retreat.

Tonpa Shenrab Miwo: the founder of Bön.

torma: hand-molded ornaments made of butter and barley flour, used as offerings in religious ceremonies.

Trisong Detsen: 8th-century Tibetan king, who, together with Padmasambhava, helped to establish Buddhism in Tibet.

trithang: a type of thangka in which the sacred image is painted.

tsa-tsa: a small, votive painted-clay tablet depicting a Tibetan Buddhist deity or great master.

Tsongkhapa: 14th-century founder of the Gelug school of Tibetan Buddhism.

tulku: an incarnate master.

Vajrayana: lit.: "diamond vehicle," a Buddhist path practiced by Tibetan Buddhists, based on tantric texts; *see tantra*.

Vinaya: the rules of monastic life.

Virupa: a 9th-century Indian adept, originator of *Lamdre*.

yana: lit. "vehicle." The three *yanas* are Hinayana, Mahayana, and Vajrayana.

Yarlung Empire: Tibetan dynasty extending from early 7th–late 9th century, during which Tibet ruled large portions of Central Asia

Yeshe O: an 11th-century Tibetan king who invited Atisha to Tibet.

yoga: specifically, a Hindu discipline meant to unite the individual with the divine; more generally, can refer to any such spiritual path.

yogi: in Tibetan Buddhism, refers to a meditator who has spent extensive time in retreat, as well as a practitioner of yoga.

Zho-tan: a midsummer yogurt festival held in Lhasa.

RESOURCES & BIBLIOGRAPHY

WEBSITES

The Tibet Fund: www.tibetfund.org
The Tibet Fund is the principal fundraising organization for Tibetan refugees. Since their founding under the auspices of H.H. the Dalai Lama over 20 years ago, hardly a day goes by in which the lives of the Tibetan community are not touched by the sustaining activities of The Tibet Fund. Through its programs, The Tibet Fund provides humanitarian relief to thousands of Tibetans who have undertaken the dangerous journey to freedom, so they can rebuild their lives; it provides food, shelter, medical care, and clean water for the elderly and children—many of whom are orphaned or suffering from debilitating ailments. The Tibet Fund also supports educational, economic, and cultural programs in an endeavor to preserve the imperiled Tibetan culture, which has done so much to enrich the world. To make a donation, visit their website or call/write to: 241 E. 32nd Street, NYC 10016; 212-213-5011.

Official site of The Government of Tibet in Exile: www.tibet.com

BOOKS

Allione, Tsultrim. *Women of Wisdom*. New York: Snowlion Publications, 2000.

Chö Yang, Year of Tibet Edition. Dharamsala: Council for Religious and Public Affairs of H.H. the Dalai Lama, 1991.

Chögyam Trungpa Rinpoche. *Visual Dharma: The Buddhist Art of Tibet*. Berkeley: Shambhala Publications Inc., 1975.

Coleman, Graham. *A Handbook of Tibetan Culture*. Boston: Shambhala Publications Inc., 1974.

Olivier and Danielle Föllmi, and Matthieu Ricard. *Buddhist Himalayas*. New York: Harry N. Abrams, Inc., 2002.

Gyatso, Tenzin (14th Dalai Lama). *The World of Tibetan Buddhism*. Boston: Wisdom Publications, 1995.

Johnathan Landaw and Andy Weber. *Images of Enlightenment: Tibetan Art in Practice*. New York: Snowlion Publications, 1993.

Mullin, Glenn H. *The Fourteen Dalai Lamas: A Sacred Legacy of Reincarnation*. Santa Fe: Clear Light Publishers, 2001.

Novick, Rebecca McClen. *Fundamentals of Tibetan Buddhism*. Freedom, CA: The Crossing Press, 1999.

Powers, John. *Introduction to Tibetan Buddhism*. New York: Snowlion Publications, 1995.

Reynolds, Valrae. *From the Sacred Realm: Treasures of Tibetan Art from the Newark Museum*. Munich: Prestel Verlag, 1999.

Sogyal Rinpoche. *The Tibetan Book of Living and Dying*. New York: HarperCollins, 1993.

Thurman, Robert. *Essential Tibetan Buddhism*. Edison, NJ: Castle Books, 1997.

Tung, Rosemary Jones. *A Portrait of Lost Tibet*. Berkeley: University of California Press, 1980.

INDEX

PHOTOGRAPHY CREDITS

Every effort has been made to acknowledge all copyright holders. However should any photograph not be correctly attributed, the publisher will undertake any appropriate changes in future editions of the book.

t=top; b=bottom; l=left; r=right; c=center

DON FARBER
1–14, 15c, 19br, 20–22, 23b, 24, 25t, 26, 27c, 27tl, 28–35, 37tr & 37br, 39tr, 40–41, 42bl, 44tr, 44–45c, 45tr, 46–53, 58–89, 90b, 91b, 92–93, 95t, 96, 100–112, 113t, 114–24, 125br, 126–31, 136–45, 146–47c, 147tr & 147b, 148–65, 167–70, 171br, 172–75, 176bl, 177tr, 179br, 180bl, 181tr, 182–84

CORBIS
15br, 125tl © Lindsay Hebberd/CORBIS; 18cl © Bennett Dean Eye Ubiquitous/CORBIS; 18–19c © CORBIS; 36–37c, 95b, 133, 135tr, 180tl © Galen Rowell/CORBIS; 38t © Bill Wassman/CORBIS; 38b, 181tl © Dean Conger/CORBIS; 39b © Wolfgang Kaehler/CORBIS; 42tl, 42–43c, 56tr, 57tr, 146cl © Bettmann/CORBIS; 54tl, 94, 99br, 180bl © Craig Lovell/CORBIS; 43t, 44bl, 54b, 55tr © Hulton-Deutsch Collection/CORBIS; 55bl © Charles & Josette Lenars/CORBIS; 91t © Liang Zhuoming/CORBIS; 97 © Tom Nebbia/CORBIS; 98-99 © Royalty-Free/CORBIS; 125tr © Christine Kolisch/CORBIS; 132 © Tiziana and Gianni Baldizzone/CORBIS; 134t © ROBERT Van den Berge/CORBIS SYGMA; 135b © David Samuel Robbins/CORBIS; 166tr © Underwood & Underwood/CORBIS; 166b © Michael S. Yamashita/CORBIS; 171t © Michael Freeman/CORBIS; 176tr © Daniel Lainé/CORBIS; 177b © Macduff Everton/CORBIS; 155br, 180–181c © Alison Wright/CORBIS

ADDITIONAL PHOTOGRAPHY
Courtesy of the Shelley & Donald Rubin Foundation: 14cl, 15tr, 20bl; Courtesy of the Shelley & Donald Rubin Collection: 17tr, 23tr, 25br, 26tl (Himalayan Art Project / www.tibetart.com)

Collection Geshe Tenzin Wangyal Rinpoche, Ligmincha Institute: 16bl, 16-17c, 17bl

36bl © Ernst Haas/Getty Images

56bl © Anna Keldon

57b © DIIR/Tibet Images (www.tibetimages.co.uk)

113b, 134b, 178–179t © The Newark Museum / Art Resource, NY

ACKNOWLEDGMENTS

Author's Acknowledgments

While my name is attached to this book, it would be a mistake to give the impression that this is one person's work. This project has truly been a collective effort, perhaps more like a film than a book, and the list of the credits is longer than I have space to record. But there are several people whose support and involvement have been pivotal. My editor Barbara Berger was so much more than an editor. It was she who really spearheaded the book, brilliantly guiding what was a challenging and complex project. She often worked late into the night, advising, researching, editing, and writing with her colleague Jennifer Williams, while staving off the ever-impending deadlines with remarkable finesse. A huge part of the project was organizing the images, and from them developing a photo essay. In this endeavor, I would like to extend my gratitude to Barbara and to DK's art director, Dirk Kaufman, who designed the beautiful jacket and oversaw the outstanding interior design created by Sherry Williams and Tilman Reitzle, of Oxygen Design. At DK Publishing, I am also grateful to publisher Chuck Lang, creative director Tina Vaughan, project director Sharon Lucas, category publisher Jonathan Metcalf, subsidiary rights manager Audrey Puzzo, contracts manager Gregor Hall, production manager Chris Avgherinos, DTP designer Milos Orlovic, and publicity director Cathy Melnicki. I am also indebted to Patricia Gift, at One Spirit Book Club, for her gracious enthusiasm and support of this project. Once the pictures were agreed upon, we were faced with the daunting task of developing the text, and brought in Rebecca Novick, author of *Fundamentals of Tibetan Buddhism,* to help write. We worked electronically, zipping documents back and forth between New York and L.A., as if we were all sitting together as a team of writers, creating a remarkable working experience. There will inevitably be some mistakes within these pages, and perhaps some misunderstandings, but these will hopefully be outweighed by the book's positive effects.

Other key people include Joanie Choderow, who edited many of the interviews, and Laurie Beth Kay, who helped with transcribing them. I would also like to thank Choegon Rinpoche, who provided information on Buddhism in Himachal Pradesh; Rinchen Dharlo, from The Tibet Fund, who gave tremendous support; Dorji Kunthup, from the Office of Tibet in New York, who kindly reviewed the text; and Jeff Watt, of the Rubin Foundation, for his expert advice. I am also very grateful to Venerable Lobsang Tsultrim, who did the exquisite calligraphy, and Venerable Geshe Gyeltsen, who answered questions when needed.

There are a number of individuals and organizations who helped in various ways to support my photography and research of Tibetan Buddhist life. I am grateful to the J. William Fulbright Foreign Scholarship Board for their major support. Important support also came from A&I Color Lab, the Buddhist Association of Taipei, Bukyo Dendo Kyokai USA, the Asian Cultural Council, Eastman Kodak Company, Teikyoku Security Patrol Company, and NPA Printing. I am also grateful to the following individuals: David Blundell, Gary Garrison, Hy Farber, Rose Farber, Yeshi Chozom Farber, Tenzin Geyche, Jennifer Greenfield, Joe Hawk, Ven. Kuang Hsin, Ish Ishihara, Rob Jacobs, Kim Kapin, Rev. Takashi Kiuchi, Irv and the late Rose Kramer, Lew Lancaster, the late Tony Leitner, Teri Lim, Tano Maida, Rajni Nair, Lama Ngawang, Donald Rubin, Yutaka Takahana, Tsering Tashi, Lhundup Tseten, Nicholas Vreeland, Tsering Wangyal, Kitty White, Ken Yang, Bob Zaugh, and Hanna Zylberberg,

Publisher's Acknowledgments

DK Publishing would like to thank the following people: Don Farber, for bringing this special project to us, for sharing his remarkable photographic treasures and knowledge of Buddhism, and for his inspiring words and boundless dedication to scholarship. For their invaluable support, we are especially grateful to Rinchen Dharlo, president of the Tibet Fund; Patricia Gift, Editor-in-Chief, One Spirit Book Club; and Dorji Kunthup, Office of Tibet. We offer special thanks to Rebecca Novick, for her tireless efforts and excellent text; and Sherry Williams and Tilman Reitzle at Oxygen Design, for their stunning design and for pulling rabbits out of hats every time.

This book would not have been possible without the assistance and efforts of people from many institutions who supplied photography and expertise, for which we are grateful—Jeff Watt, at The Shelley & Donald Rubin Foundation, and Emily Malinowsky, at The Shelley & Donald Rubin Cultural Trust, New York; Lee Hartline, Sue Davis, and Tenzin Wangyal Rinpoche, at the Ligmincha Institute, Charlottesville, VA; Valrae Reynolds and Scott Hankins, the Newark Museum; Jemal Creary, Corbis; photographer Anna Kelden; Valerie Zars, Getty Images; Ian Cumming, Tibet Images; Ryan Jensen, Art Resources; Ellen Applebee; and Leslie DiRusso. We are also grateful to Josephine and Catherine Yam, Colourscan, for the stunning reproductions; Nanette Cardon, IRIS, for her superb index; Miesha Tate for assisting with the design; and Beth Hester, Anja Schmidt, John Searcy, Lucas Mansell, and Jane Perlmutter, for their editorial help.